RENT

First published in 2000 by
Marino Books
an imprint of Mercier Press
16 Hume Street Dublin 2
Tel: (01) 661 5299; Fax: (01) 661 8583
E.mail: books@marino.ie

Trade enquiries to CMD Distribution
55A Spruce Avenue
Stillorgan Industrial Park
Blackrock County Dublin
Tel: (01) 294 2556; Fax: (01) 294 2564
E.mail: cmd@columba.ie

© Evanna Kearins 2000

ISBN 1 86023 107 1

10 9 8 7 6 5 4 3 2 1

A CIP record for this title is available
from the British Library

Cover design by SPACE
Printed in Ireland by ColourBooks
Baldoyle Dublin 13

RENT

THE UNTOLD STORY
OF MALE PROSTITUTION IN DUBLIN

EVANNA KEARINS

ACKNOWLEDGEMENTS

There are so many people that I would like to thank for their help in the production of this book. I would firstly like to thank Brian Trench for his help and kindness during the formulation of the idea of this study and Colum Kenny for his supervision as the idea gathered momentum. Thank you Colum for your advice, encouragement, constructive criticism and for your concern for my safety as I entered the unknown. I would also like to thank Peadar Kirby.

To my parents, Micéal and Frances, for their unwavering support, love and patience over the years. I hope with all my heart that I will continue to make them proud and that some day I will be able to repay them a fraction of the kindness that they have shown to me. To my sister Valerie for reading each chapter of this book on completion and for taking me out on a very regular basis. To my brother Karl for making the initial contacts for me. Thanks are also due to my eldest brother, Adrian, his wife, Louise, and my niece and nephew, Eirinn and Connell.

A special thanks to the gardaí who took the time to speak to me. To Gerry Curran for coming with me on my first visit to the Phoenix Park in the early hours of the morning. To Paddy O'Gorman for all the useful information that he gave to me. To Jarlath Taheny for his friendship and support. To Mark O'Sullivan for the photographs in this book – for his kindness, his talent and his patience; to Peter Diamond for his computer expertise, to Pat Conroy and to all my friends in the Today FM newsroom.

To my friends Niamh, Ursula, Gillian, Louise, Karen, Gráinne, Julie, Amanda (for phoning me almost every day), Jenny, Sharon, Lisa, Helen, Sheila, Orla, Ruth, Eimer, Anne Marie, Caitriona, Deirdre, Peter, Damien, John Egan, Paul, Padraig, David, Fintan, Kevin, Gerry, Mick, Anne and Paula. Without you all, life would be very dull.

I would like to thank everyone whom I interviewed as part of my research. My greatest debt is to the male prostitutes, without whom this research would have been impossible. Thank you for your honesty, your trust and your openness. I hope that I have given you all a fair voice and I extend my deepest thanks to you.

Other contacts and interviewees to whom thanks are due include Mick Quinlan (Gay Men's Health Project), Fr Peter McVerry, barrister Raymond Byrne, James O'Connor (OpenHeart House), Niamh Moynihan (Cairde), Dr Art O'Connor (Central Mental Hospital), Richard Balls (the *Irish Times*), Paul Flynn (Crosscare), Feargal McDonagh (chaplain, Arbour Hill Prison), *Gay Community News*, Noel (Outhouse), Focus Ireland and the Merchants Quay Project.

What Am I?

I am an ordinary man
That's what I am
I may be gay
but I'm still a man
Society hates me
and wants to get rid of me
Why do they detest me so?
I am an ordinary man
A prostitute is really what I am
I sell sex for money
Why is that so bad?
I am an ordinary man
Please accept me for what I am
(Paul, self-employed masseur)

*I would like to dedicate this book to all those
who see male prostitution as their only means of survival.*

Contents

INTRODUCTION

If you want to learn more about a marginalised, disen-franchised, criminalised and misunderstood section of Irish society, then this book is for you. It provides a vivid account of the lives of male prostitutes in Dublin, ranging from those at street level to those involved in covert or off-street prostitution. Interspersed throughout the book are a number of life stories, which illustrate and bring to life the typical everyday experiences of male sex workers in Dublin.

My intention is not to expose those involved in male prostitution – all names and identifying information have been changed in order to protect the confidentiality of the participants – nor to put them out of business, nor to shock the reader, but to explore a world which is largely ignored and misconstrued in Ireland. I hope that this book will raise awareness of male prostitution in Dublin and encourage the establishment of services designed to help those who are involved in it. I hope that more will be done to help these people to seek better life alternatives in the near future.

I would like to apologise for any language which may be considered offensive in this book, but it is my intention to tell the story from the male prostitutes' point of view, using their language as far as possible.

The interview was the most important element of the research I did for this book. Interviews were conducted over a period of nine months (from October 1998 to June 1999). I also analysed books, articles and other texts relating to the topic. Most of the literature I obtained is from the US and the UK. I found only one survey, conducted by the Gay Men's Health Project (GMHP), on male prostitution in Ireland. The literature-review process was quite lengthy, as the bibliography will illustrate, but it was absolutely necessary in order to obtain a full understanding of how male prostitution in Ireland compares to the profession in the US and the UK, for example.

It is very difficult to determine the numbers of male prostitutes in Dublin because of the 'underground' nature of the profession, but I think that there may be far more involved than any of us would care to believe. The initial process of engaging male prostitutes for interview was complex and required a great deal of perseverance. Once the initial contacts were made and the purpose of the research outlined, most of the men and the boys were happy to take part. Care was taken to minimise distortion and to ensure confidentiality. This was particularly important to all the male prostitutes and was essential if they were to discuss candidly matters involving embarrassing or awkward situations. Follow-up interviews were arranged as far as possible, especially if there was any hint of fabrication in the first interview. This permitted me to verify any questionable information. It also enabled me to develop a sense of trust and openness, which empowered me to probe deeper into more sensitive areas.

My research was restricted to male sex workers who cater to male clients only. Interviews were conducted with five 'street' prostitutes (rent boys) and six 'off-street' workers, including three male masseurs, two escorts, one man who meets his clients in gay saunas in the city centre and one man who worked as a rent boy in London thirty years ago. The men ranged in age from eighteen to forty-nine years, with the majority in the twenty- to twenty-five-year-old category. Most of the street prostitutes were unemployed, having left school before completing the Leaving Certificate. The majority of those involved in 'street' prostitution had been homeless for some period of their lives. Of the off-street prostitutes, most were well-educated; three had attended university. All of the off-street prostitutes identified themselves as gay or bisexual, while most of the street workers stated that they were heterosexual. The off-street respondents ranged from those with effeminate mannerisms and camp expressions to those with a very macho physiognomy. Most of the male prostitutes were from Dublin – just two were originally from outside Dublin. Two of the interviewees lived at home, while some lived in flats, houses or apartments. Some were homeless, and others were staying with friends or clients. Most cited money as their main reason for involvement in male prostitution. Many of the street prostitutes spent their money on drugs and alcohol, while those in the off-street scene used the money to maintain a good standard of living. Most interviewees were helpful, volunteering details which I would have thought were embarrassing or at least compromising.

Many of the street prostitutes had suffered early emotional deprivation and some had been exposed to appalling family lives – parental squabbling, desertion, drunkenness, emotional coldness, physical violence and even sexual abuse. Few had received consistent and stable parenting during their early years. It is important to highlight the unhappy antecedents for male street prostitution.

Unfortunately, it did not prove possible to collect a sample of the clients of male prostitutes. I had to rely on the sex workers' accounts and descriptions of them.

The process of finding, meeting and interviewing the male prostitutes was interesting, frustrating at times, amusing and sometimes sad. At first I thought it would be very difficult to obtain interviews with male prostitutes in Dublin. Being unsure of the extent of the phenomenon, I was concerned that they would not be willing to speak to me. Thankfully, I was proven wrong. The interviews with the 'sex workers' were mostly face-to-face, but in one case interviews were always conducted over the phone. Some of the interviews were recorded using a Dictaphone or minidisc recorder, but in some cases I was not permitted to use any recording equipment and had to rely on note-taking.

I had reservations about paying interview fees, as I felt that doing so might affect the data collected, so I avoided this practice as far as possible. It was also necessary for me to maintain a flexible time schedule and interview subjects at their convenience (often late at night). During the interviews, I tried to develop a rapport with the male sex workers, to adopt their lingo, to be open-minded, non-judgmental and unperturbed by the content of the conversation, no matter how graphic it tended to be. This was very difficult at times. Asking questions about sexual services was often very awkward and required a great deal of sensitivity on my part. Services provided by the male prostitutes include hand relief, fellatio and anal sex. Discussing such practices in detail was often embarrassing. Many of the respondents were very sexually explicit and appeared to be unaffected by the fact that I was female. There were a few embarrassing situations for me. For instance, during an interview with Bob, a rent boy, he described the practice of 'fisting' and stopped mid-sentence and asked me if I knew what he was talking about. He then purposely described the activity in lurid detail, finding my naivety an obvious source of amusement. I also had to become accustomed to the kind of specialist lingo that male street prostitutes, in particular, tend to use on a regular basis, for example 'fisting', 'BJs' for blow jobs, 'S&M' for sadomasochism, 'foy' for methadone and so on.

Locations for interviewing the male prostitutes varied depending on whether they were street or off-street workers. Mark (rent boy) was interviewed on many occasions, once in a garda station, once in my car, once in a room in Dublin City University and twice in the Phoenix Park. Brian (rent boy) was interviewed twice in the Phoenix Park. Bob (rent boy) was interviewed in a café on two occasions and Robert (rent boy) was interviewed twice over the phone. Donal was interviewed in his home. I met Thomas (escort) in a pub, Joe (meets clients in gay saunas), Frank (escort), Paul and David (self-employed masseurs) in their homes, and Stephen in a café. While I interviewed only four rent boys and one former rent boy in detail, I spoke briefly to others and observed many of them at work, both in the Phoenix Park and on Burgh Quay. These respondents also gave me detailed information on their clients and on those men who operate as pimps.

My first visit to the Phoenix Park was at midnight on a Thursday night. For me this was a very frightening and unnerving experience, as I was entering the unknown. Even though I was accompanied by two male friends and dressed like a boy, this was a very dangerous and perhaps unwise undertaking – the level of crime is very high in the Phoenix Park. We witnessed 'pick-ups' by a number of clients (who were mostly middle-aged), two men having sex in a car by the Polo Grounds and another couple having sex by the trees near the Magazine Hill.

The outsider entering the male prostitute's world for the first time will be confronted with a world turned inside out, a sub-world where everyday events and transactions lose their usual significance. 'Normality' becomes distorted, and the familiar badges of masculinity and heterosexuality are discarded. In such a context, I was often the outsider, as both a researcher and a woman. Initially, the whole situation was not only confusing but rather frightening, as I entered the homes of male prostitutes, not knowing what awaited me inside. I took great risks, some would say foolishly, but fortunately I have managed to come through the experience completely unharmed. While there were times when I felt uncomfortable, most of the male prostitutes that I met were very friendly and open once they had accepted me.

1

'On the Game'

MALE PROSTITUTION IN DUBLIN

'Prostitution', or the selling and buying of sex, is a harsh word loaded with condemnatory tones. It is a means of earning or supplementing a living for many men and women worldwide and is usually associated with poverty. Prostitution is not just a product of our turbulent era but a widespread activity, which is often referred to as 'the world's oldest profession'. The history of male and female prostitution goes back to references in early literature, plays, poems, murals and other works of art.

Little public concern has been expressed regarding the perceived growth in male prostitution in Dublin because very little is known about it. Prostitution is generally perceived to be a woman's occupation, but male prostitution is probably as old as the female variety. It is only relatively recently that the public perception of prostitutes as women and girls expanded to include men. Male prostitutes in Ireland constitute an extremely under-identified, under-served and all too often misinterpreted population. The lack of recognition of this subculture is determined largely by a constellation of societal myths or beliefs regarding what it means to be male and straight in Irish society. There are few forms of behaviour that are more rife with myth, folklore and assumptions than male prostitution. The Bible is often seen as the basis for the dominant views on homosexuality and prostitution.

The sex industry is flourishing in Ireland, as it is in other countries. There are no official statistics as to how many men are involved in it and numbers are difficult to gauge because some males drift in and out of 'the game'. Nonetheless, it is clear that male prostitution is big business in Dublin and there are indications that there are clusters of it right across the city. Estimates of the number of male prostitutes in Dublin, received from the many service providers interviewed, range from 100 to 600.

Prostitution covers a range of behaviours and groups. I have defined male prostitution as follows: 'Male prostitution occurs when any male provides sexual services for another male and receives payment or other material benefit in return.' The definition purposely refers to 'any male': that means any male of any sexual orientation, be he heterosexual, homosexual or bisexual. There is a common perception that those involved in male prostitution are exclusively homosexual but that is not always the case. A heterosexual male may engage in sexual activity with another male for a number of reasons. It is important to state that the 'payment' need not be a monetary transaction but could be a place to stay, something to eat, clothes, protection or drugs.

The obsession in Irish society with labelling, based on who you are having sex with, poses many problems for those who do not conform. The man who has sex with another man for money but is not gay is seen as an alien creature because he is outside the existing structures of heterosexual and homosexual. The straight hustler is caught in a contradiction. Even though he engages regularly in homosexual acts in the economically inferior role of prostitute, he wishes to retain a dominant, masculine, heterosexual self-image. This male copes with the contradiction by making money, which neutralises his sense of repulsion at what he is doing.

It is also important to make a distinction between homosexuals, who 'cruise', and male prostitutes, who 'trawl'. Homosexual cruising involves meeting sexual partners in the public territories of the male homosexual subculture, but this does not involve the exchange of money for sex. The homosexual and the prostitute are two very different people with dissimilar motives.

The street prostitute may be homosexual, heterosexual, bisexual or undecided about his sexual identity. Many of the rent boys that I met identified themselves as heterosexuals and vehemently denied any homosexual tendencies, probably because of the stigma that is still attached to homosexuality in Ireland. Heterosexual males may become involved in male prostitution because of a pressing need for money; easy money overcomes their distaste for the homosexual act. It may be suggested that long-term involvement in male prostitution can affect the male prostitute's sexual orientation, causing him to develop personal homosexual desires, but this is unproven as a hypothesis. Many street hustlers tend to exaggerate and defend their masculinity, insisting that they do not have full anal sex and that they are heterosexual. They tend to perceive what they are doing as a business transaction rather than a sexual encounter. They feel the need to protect their masculinity because of homosexual prejudice.

Of the prostitutes whom I interviewed, five professed themselves to be homosexual, four heterosexual and two bisexual. It is not possible to say how typical or representative the eleven men I spoke to are of Dublin prostitutes in general.

I have loosely defined two categories of male prostitute – street and off-street – but it is important to remember that these classifications are not rigid and should not be looked upon as such, because male prostitutes may change their roles and are highly flexible, adaptable and opportunistic. Street prostitutes include boys or men working the streets on foot, who are commonly referred to as 'rent boys' or 'chickens'. This is seen as the lower end of the market. Off-street prostitutes include masseurs, escorts and those male prostitutes who 'fraternise' in some gay saunas around the city. Off-street is seen as the top end of the market and can take place in commercial outlets such as escort agencies, saunas or massage parlours or in the prostitute's or client's home. It can be very profitable and operates under the guise of a legitimate business. Some prostitutes start out on the street and seek advancement to off-street prostitution.

There are a number of factors that distinguish private from public prostitution. These two broad groups differ in their style of operation, the services they offer, the type of clients they attract and the kind of backgrounds the prostitutes come from. Collectively, I will refer to the street workers and off-street workers as 'hustlers', which includes many different kinds of people with varying sexual orientations and degrees of involvement. They can be heterosexual, homosexual or bisexual and temporary, occasional or continual prostitutes. 'Sex worker' is another polite term used to describe those who sell their bodies, both on and off the street. This term acknowledges the fact that prostitution can be seen as a form of work. It also serves to link street prostitutes politically with others in the sex industry, for example, off-street workers such as masseurs and escorts.

Street prostitution is a casual occupation, in that the hustlers and clients meet by chance, without pre-arrangement. The agreement is usually made out of doors in public places such as the Phoenix Park, Burgh Quay, in public toilets or in the client's car. Sexual services range from mutual masturbation to fellatio or 'blow jobs' and insertive or receptive anal intercourse. As a result of the public nature of street prostitution, the client and hustler may be restricted to those sexual activities that will enable them to make a quick getaway should an intrusion occur. The majority of street prostitutes appear to be working-class and many of them are homeless, having run away from or been thrown out of their homes. Those who still live at home seem not to have a stable family environment. Street prostitutes have often drifted into the sex industry as a result of a desperate shortage of money, whether for food, shelter, clothes or drugs.

The fees charged by street prostitutes in Dublin depend on the type of service provided, but they generally range from £10 to £25 for mutual masturbation (active or passive 'hand relief' or a 'hand job') and active or passive fellatio to £50 to £70 for full anal sex (which may be insertive or receptive). The prices also depend on the kind of 'punters', or customers, involved. Street prostitutes tend to cater for middle-aged or older men (thirty to seventy years old) who are often married with children. They may be inherently homosexual, having been unable to accept their sexual orientation at the time of their marriage. Homosexuals who

23

purchase hustlers' services are often older, unattractive and socially inadequate men or those who seek unusual or highly erotic sex.

Working on the streets can expose the male prostitute to many dangers – such as entrapment by the gardaí, physical violence and robbery – which the off-street prostitutes find easier to avoid. The street prostitute requires no capital to begin work as accommodation and special equipment are not prerequisites for obtaining clients. The trade is therefore viable for those young boys who are homeless and unemployed, and for their customers it seems that the younger these boys are, the better.

Access to off-street prostitution is usually restricted to those who can afford to have their own home. They are generally better educated and often identify as homosexual or bisexual, choosing to become involved in prostitution rather than being forced into it by economic necessity. This group includes the masseurs, escorts and male prostitutes who operate from some gay saunas. The masseurs are usually self-employed but some work in massage parlours. If they are self-employed, they arrange their own clients, mainly through advertisements in the gay press, and are free from the control of an agency. They generally work in their own homes or those of their clients and provide a full range of sexual services, as well as massages. The contract is formed between the client and the prostitute over the phone and rates are usually similar to those charged by the agencies but higher than those charged by the street prostitutes. The prices range from £40 for massage only, £60 for massage and oral sex and up to £150-£200 for full anal sex. Occasionally, clients require only a massage. They range in age from eighteen to sixty years and may include covert bisexuals, i.e. married men seeking occasional anonymous sexual contact, and openly gay identified men.

The escort works for an agency that takes a proportion of his earnings and offers a full range of sexual services in his or the client's home. Like the masseur, he tends to be better educated and more middle-class than the street prostitute. The agency acts as an intermediary between the prostitute and the client and arranges the assignation for the escort over the telephone. Those male prostitutes who frequent gay saunas may be involved in street or off-street prostitution but it is usually the latter. There are a number of gay saunas in the Dublin area and while they are primarily used as saunas by homosexuals, it appears to be the case that male prostitutes often avail of the privacy and anonymity which they allow in order to meet their clients.

Other types of male prostitute have been identified, such as 'kept boys', where the hustler provides sexual services in return for shelter, food, clothing etc. As I have no solid information on this group, they will not be referred to in any great detail.

There are a number of factors that leave young people vulnerable to becoming involved in selling sex. The widespread belief is that males become involved in prostitution primarily for financial gain. 'Sure it's easy money, and it's tax-free, where would I make that kind of money in a straight job?' (Brian, bisexual rent boy).

Homelessness is clearly a factor in some instances. According to a survey compiled by Dublin Simon soup run, Focus Ireland and staff from Dublin Corporation during the week 21–27 June 1998, 12 per cent of homeless people in Dublin are under eighteen years, 37 per cent are under twenty-five years and 77 per cent are male. Once out on the streets, these young people's options are limited to begging, prostitution and acquisitive crime. Inadequate social policies in this country contribute to young males entering prostitution and militate against young males leaving the trade. It is of course understood that the majority of runaway and homeless boys do not become involved in prostitution, and it is clear that a number of factors besides financial need contribute to entry into the profession. Male prostitution may be experienced as a form of stability, without the apparent restrictions and rules of conventional work.

Peer pressure and drug and alcohol addiction may also be among the reasons for entering prostitution. Often the rent boy goes on the game to feed his drug habit. Many street prostitutes are using a wide range of drugs that may be injected or taken orally. This group is extremely vulnerable and requires immediate intervention from health professionals.

Sexual abuse in childhood is often seen as a cause of male prostitution. Bolton et al. (1989) regard prostitution as simply a continuation of earlier abusive sex. However, establishing a direct causal relationship between prostitution and sexual abuse remains controversial. In my opinion, a combination of adverse influences rather than just sexual abuse causes entry into the sex trade. While two of the street prostitutes that I interviewed had experienced early sexual abuse, they were also victims of childhood adversity, neglect and emotional conflict. There are a number of landmarks on the road to prostitution and there is no sole cause.

Some of the boys who tell their stories in this book were exploited by men, through a process of friendship and seduction, until consent to the sexual act was gradually won. Compliance was rewarded with gifts, drugs or money. In this way, boys may be introduced into the prostitution subculture. Some boys may be starved of adult affection and attention and may feel loved and wanted by their clients. Not all street prostitutes are repulsed by the sexual activity involved and some are homosexual in their orientation. There is, however, a general reluctance to profess openly that one is gay in street prostitution circles.

The most common reasons cited to me for involvement in male prostitution included lack of money, homelessness (poverty), unemployment, drugs/alcohol abuse, poor family background/abuse, sexual or physical abuse, desire for attention/companionship, sex or a combination of these factors. There are a number of positive 'pull' factors and negative 'push' factors that encourage and prevent involvement in male prostitution. There are strong incentives to remain in prostitution – it can be lucrative, hours are flexible, and at the top end of the market there is a certain glamour, such as luxurious surroundings, a good standard of living and so on. The negative, push factors which might prevent involvement in male prostitution include health risks; the dangers involved, such as physical and sexual abuse, robberies or even murder; coming into contact with the law; family intolerance and rejection on finding out about the nature of the person's work; and loss of self-esteem.

Brian, one of the rent boys I interviewed, attempted to explain his reasons for becoming a male street prostitute:

> I was told to leave home because I was always
> in trouble, at home, at school and even with
> the law. I ended up on the streets with
> nothing. I was sixteen years old and scared

shitless. I didn't know what to be doing and I had to look after myself, you know, and find places to stay and all. I had no food or nothing. I used to beg and steal a little at first but I still wasn't surviving. I met some other guys who was on the game in the Park [Phoenix Park] and they were the same age as myself and they says they were making a packet so I says to myself I'll give that a go. I had to go along – it was either that or starve. I was desperate and I just gave it a go. I just got into it and all I did after that.

Once involved, many male prostitutes become addicted to the lifestyle and to the amount of money they make and often find it very difficult to leave it for conventional work. The main areas of male prostitution in Dublin include the Phoenix Park or any park in Dublin, Burgh Quay, the alleyway near Dublin Castle, public toilets, some city-centre pubs and clubs, some massage parlours, escort agencies, the hustler's or the client's home, gay saunas, some hotels and B&Bs. There has been little talk of male prostitution in Ireland and the scarcity of literature available on the subject highlights the fact that it is generally ignored in this country. Media attention focused on the subject around the time that a particular politician was discovered in the Phoenix Park in March 1994, but this attention was short-lived.

2

'This Is My Life'

MARK'S STORY

Mark is a twenty-two-year-old, single rent boy. He can be seen almost daily hustling in the Phoenix Park, while at night he can be seen around Burgh Quay. He became homeless and started 'on the game' when he was fifteen, returning home for one year when he was sixteen. He left home again when he was seventeen and has never returned. Mark has had a very unhappy family life as a result of physical, emotional and sexual abuse. He comes from a working-class background and is one of eight children. In his early years, two of his cousins also lived in the family's four-bedroom council house. Both his mother and father have a drink problem, and Mark was often physically abused by his belligerent, authoritarian and homophobic father. His mother appears to be weak, submissive and unconcerned about her son's welfare. Mark was sexually abused by one of his cousins (his maternal uncle's son) when he was nine or ten years of age. The abuse included fondling and oral sex. When he was twelve years old, he was sodomised by an older boy in his neighbourhood. Mark feels that there may be a causal connection between the sexual abuse to which he was subjected as a child and his entry into prostitution.

Mark bears the worst scars of a street kid. He is a chronic heroin addict of no fixed abode. He occasionally stays with one of his brothers, some friends or with clients. He is very streetwise and knows how to look after himself. He has sandy-coloured, neatly cut hair and blue eyes. He is undernourished, thin, weather-beaten and uncared-for. He is most often seen wearing dirty blue jeans, a hooded pullover, runners and a baseball cap. His clothes are dirty but usually fashionable. He rarely wears a coat. He is not very attractive and most of his teeth are rotten due to heroin abuse and lack of care. He spends most of his days outdoors. When he is not hustling, he can be seen wandering around the city.

Mark has a very good personality but is not willing to trust other people. When allowed to shine, he has a great sense of humour and loves to laugh, although he does so reluctantly. He also lacks affection and emotional support. He says there is no one in this world who he can trust. His future does not look very bright and he does not believe that he will live very long.

When I first met Mark, he was quiet. He refused to look me in the eye and thought of me as a way of making money. He wanted me to pay him for the interview. It took some time to get him to talk freely, but once he began, talking seemed to have a therapeutic effect on him. The tough Mark was temporarily replaced by a boy who was longing for someone to listen to him. We met on a number of occasions in the Phoenix Park and on each occasion he seemed prepared to disclose more about himself. On our last meeting, he seemed sad and admitted he would miss our conversations. He knows all the boys on the game in the Park but is not very close to any of them. Mark finds it difficult to maintain eye contact while holding a conversation. He tends to keep his head down, directing his eyes towards the ground. He also tends to use his hands a lot while speaking. He is obsessed with money and making money and is always worried that one day he will not make enough to buy drugs.

Mark claims to be heterosexual and seems to despise those who are homosexual. He seemed determined to prove his heterosexuality. He has two children of his own whom he never sees because he is no longer in touch with their mother. Mark was introduced to the male sex industry by a much older man after he left home the first time. This is a first-hand account of his life:

'There was a lot of grief goin' on in the house, you know. Me Ma and Da are heavy into the drink and anytime I came in I was gettin' gave out and it wasn't just me either, it was the rest of the family as well. There was eight of us in our family and me Ma's brother's two sons were livin' in our house, you know, two of them . . . me cousin Chubby was stayin' with us years ago and he was like gay and all, you know. I think he's locked up in England now for child molestin' [pause]. When I was a kid he used to sit beside me real close like and his hand would be beside me and he'd be like that, you know, lettin' on to rub his leg, but he'd be touchin' my leg, you know, to see how I'd react. I hadn't a clue at the time . . . I was only nine or ten when I woke up one mornin' and found him sittin' on the bed beside me with his yoke in his hand; me trousers were down around me ankles and me T-shirt was up high and like his trousers were off him and there was all bleedin'

31

sticky stuff all over me stomach like, you know, and I didn't know what the fuck it was at the time. I know now like, you know, that fucker had come all over me, he was after being messin' around with me when I was asleep . . . I honestly think that that might be affectin' what I'm doin' now, because another time I called down to a friend and I was about twelve at the time and his brother answered the door, he did. I do still see him to this day and I went into the house to wait for Thomas. His brother said he was in the toilet and told me to sit down on the chair. He grabbed me, he did, put me down over the armchair, took me trousers down and you know, I was like, Jaysus, what's he doin' to me, where's Thomas, you know, lookin' for his brother and he just pulled down me pants and put his yoke between me legs, pushin' it into me arse and started movin' up and down. I remember it was awful sore. Then a knock came to the door and he says to me, "Quick, quick, get your trousers up and get out over the back, hurry", as if I had done somethin', you know what I mean. It was bleedin' him attacked me but I never said anythin' to anyone about it, you know.

'Thinkin' back on it, it had some effect on what I'm doin' like, you know. Don't get me wrong. I don't enjoy what I do. I do it for the money like, that's all – the money . . . I never told me family about me cousin either 'cos all me brothers know that he is gay like and he used to go out drinkin' with them, he did, this is goin' back now a few year ago, and they were drinkin' one day in Oriel Park and they were all drunk and somethin' happened between me brother, Fintan, and me cousin. Fintan told me other brother and he battered him. Me brother flipped, he did, he battered him and ended up stabbin' him in the arm, he fuckin' bet the shit out of him

32

and he ended up fuckin' off to England and the last we heard was he was locked up over there for child molestin' . . .

'I left school after me confirmation when I was thirteen. I didn't go to school much anyways. I was kept back in school 'cos I was a bit slow at learnin' things like, you know. I'm not even the best of a reader like. After I left school, anythin' was setting them off. You could do nothin' right – they were never happy. When me Da was drinkin', he'd be gettin' all heavy and all, he'd be givin' out to me and callin' me scumbag and all that and lookin' for a fight. Then if I said anythin' at all like, you know, I got battered and he wouldn't stop until he'd see you were cryin' and all. He was vicious like, he was. I says, "I'm gettin' out of here, I can't take anymore", and I ended up on the streets. I met this bloke then and he owned a guest house, he did, and he took me in. He says to me, "You're out on the street, aren't ya?" He knew by lookin' at me I was. I thought he was a great bloke until he ripped me off. I used to live with him and he took care of me, he did, and I had me own little room and he had me doing bits of work for him. He showed me how to do massages and all that and he started gettin' calls. People were ringin' up so I started doing massages and business like, you know. I used to have to mess around with the clients as well. You'd start the massage and then they'd start messin' around with you and you'd have to do the same to them. Some of them even wanted to be whipped and all and weird things. I was getting about £40 for the massage and I'd give half to him and keep the rest, you know, and maybe that night I'd do business with him and he let me stay on there so I introduced him to this other bloke I knew who was on the streets as well and it ended up he fucked me out and took your man in and now he's still livin' there and he's bringin' him to Spain and all and he's bringin' him everywhere.

'After that I was back on the streets with nothin' so I had heard about the Park [Phoenix Park] in the papers and all that and I heard people talkin' about rent boys and all and I used to be saying to meself "What's a rent boy?" I found out then what it was – a fella goin' up the Phoenix Park and sellin' his body for money, you know, so I says to meself, "I'll go up and try it and see what it's like", you know. I went up and started off from there then. As soon as I went up like, I stood at the railings and a fella came along on a push-bike. The first fella I was with was on a push-bike and he said "Howaya", and I says "All right." He cycled down the road and came back up and said, "Are you doin' business?" and I says, "I am" and I didn't even know how much to charge him so I says "the usual". He brought me up through the railings and went into the bushes there. We were messin' around in there. I got £25 off him, I did. We were just messin' 'round, like he wanted me to suck him off but I was like, "No, no I'm not doin' tha'", 'cos I didn't even want to be doin' any of it but I needed the money. After a while I got to meet people in cars and the people up there put me wise like as to what's goin' on, where to go and the places to be to meet punters and that's how I got started in the Park.

'Even when I went back [home] when I was sixteen, I was out of the house for a year at that stage and I'd gotten meself a job, I did. That was the only reason they took me back 'cos I was workin' and it was a great job like, making all health food like vegetarian burgers and all that like, you know. I used to work on Sundays and get double time. I was payin' £100 a week to Ma and Da and I'd be payin' off the telly and the video and they still weren't happy with no matter what you done. An English bloke took over where I was workin' and it went bankrupt so I was out of work and then they started missin' the money and started gettin' heavy again, me Da did, and I just left . . .

Me Da at that time used to be tellin' me I was a fairy and a faggot and a poof, I don't know where he got it from 'cos I'm straight and all. I'd met a bird then and we got a flat together and had two kids and she ripped me off, she did. She fucked off for a week, she did, and I was left in the house with two kids and I didn't know where she was and her family and all were ringin' me up to see where she was and she came back of a Tuesday, she did, and I says, "Where were you?" and I freaked with her, I did. I was like a madman and she said she was up in her sister's so I said, "I'm fucking goin' out now. You can watch the bleedin' kids." So I went up the road and met a few of the lads and they told me she was with this other bloke, Glen, for the week. So I went down and knocked on his door and I battered him like, you know, full of anger, I battered him. I went back to her and told her to fuck off, that we were finished and that I was going for custody. She let the flat go then, she did, and I was on the streets and under pressure 'cos I had no money to give for the kids, not workin' and all, so I ended up going back up to the Park. A few of the lads I was hangin' around with started smoking gear and I got into it as well . . . Goin' on the game keeps me habit goin' like, you know. I'm not robbin' off people or robbin' anybody's house or car. I'm makin' an honest livin'. I'm only in it for the money, it's easy money like, you know . . .

'I met a bloke once in the Park of a Sunday and he

asked me to go up the mountains with him. When we got there he said, "We'll go out of the way", so I says, "That's all right", and we went up the mountains and anyway we did and he opened the boot of the car and took out a haversack and all I was thinkin' was, "Jaysus, this fella is goin to chop me up" like, you know, you know like, he's goin to murder me. We went into the trees and he opened his bag and I was standin' a distance away like, with a big branch beside me foot just in case he tried anythin'. He started taking ropes out of the bag, Johnson's baby oil, a big whip, a big black vibrator about two foot long, no exaggeratin', and he says, "This is what I want you to do. You're all right as you are but I'm strippin' off." He took off his clothes and told me tie one hand to one tree and the other to another tree and the same with his legs and he's standin' there like all stretched open and he tells me to put baby oil on the vibrator and put it up his arse and I did and he tells me to shove it up as far as it can go. It was disgustin'. Then he tells me to get the whip and whip him and I was there like tippin' him with it like, you know, and he kept shoutin', "Harder, harder", so I hit him harder and he was lovin' it, he was, and then he tells me to light a cigarette and put it out on his back and on his dick and everywhere. I mean he was there tied to a tree with a vibrator up his arse and me there puttin' out cigarettes on him [laughs]. There were little marks all over him, little cigarette buttons all over him. He was bleedin' lovin' it, he was. This is what he got his kicks out of like, you know.

'I remember meetin' this other bloke who brought me back to his house, he did, and he opened up the wardrobe and took out his wife's weddin' dress and tells me to put it on. He said he'd give me £50 quid if I did. The more I refused the more the money went up and I put it on and anyways he gets down on his knees, underneath the dress and started blowin' me like, you know, and I felt embarrassed standin' there in a dress, but you can get asked all sorts by people. After he was finished blowin' he wanted me to come all over him. I got £70 for doin' tha'.

'I met another fella once who took me back to his place and told me to take off me jeans and leave on me boxer shorts and he says, "Let me see your toes", and I'm sayin' to meself, me bleedin' toes, you know, so I took out me toes and I'm lyin' there and he's, you know, rubbin' and kissin' and lickin' me toes and then he says, "Oh I'd love if you'd shove your big toe up me arse" and all and I'm sayin', "Ah God, is he for real" and he was like buzzin' off it like, you know, mad things they do ask you to do.

'I'd generally go up to the Park in the evenin' times in the winter around six o'clock but in the summer I'd go up much earlier, if it's a nice sunny day. I'd usually meet about three or four punters, more in summer, and could come out of there with over 200 or 300 quid some days and I'd go off and get me gear and put it into me and go off home, get up the next morning and I usually have a bit left for the next mornin' to make me feel normal and go off up the Park again and if I don't get anythin' in the Park I'll go to Burgh Quay. There'd be nights up there and you might get nothin'; there'd be no one around like and then there might be loads. On a nice sunny day, I'd go up around lunchtime and you'd get fellas up there on their lunch break. They'd fly up there on their lunch break like, you know, and go back to work and I'll head off at about three o'clock, go home and get somethin' to eat, come back up then about five o'clock, I would, and get them comin' home from work then like, you know. You get blokes passin' through comin' from work and they want to get a load off their mind. They just pick you up and you do what you can for them . . . The most I ever made in one night was 600 quid and in one week over 1,000, but that wouldn't happen very often like, you know.

'It's gettin' very dangerous now up there. A fella I know met his punter and went to the bushes near the Magazine Hill. There's a little drive-in, near the old fortress, near the hill with all the trees; there's a place we call Fantasy Land and they went in there, there's loads of bushes up there and there's a hole in it and it's like a little tree house, that's where fellas do go. These two were in there doin' the business, anyhow, and a load of blokes came in on top of them and bleedin' battered them – took everythin' off them – money, credit cards, jewellery, even took the punter's car. Queer-bashers and junkies do come up like lookin' for money, you know. They think because you are in the Park you have loads of money. If I fuckin' had loads of money, I wouldn't be bleedin' going up there like, you know. I wouldn't bleedin' be bothered. There do be fellas jumpin' out at you with baseball bats, hurley sticks, clubs, bottles, everythin' like, you know. It's gettin' that way now. You have to be carryin' money with you now, because if they don't find money, they think you are hidin' it and if they don't come across it they will just go on batterin' you until they do get somethin' off you, you know . . . There's blokes getting into cars pretendin' to be on the game and they're pullin' syringes and all on punters and it's frightenin' them off like. And even me like, you know, when I went up there first I used to walk along the road and you wouldn't even have to look behind your back and all, you know, you had no problem. If a car pulled up behind you, you knew it was a punter. The way it is now, if a car pulls in beside you, you have to look straightaway in case it's a gang like, you know.

'The punters are all sorts. Married, about in their forties or fifties; good jobs like, you know. One fella is a solicitor, another is a judge, there's another bloke I knew was a politician, there's insurance brokers and people [I've seen] on RTÉ . . . It's gettin' very public now and some punters are stayin' low and just drivin' through and when they see me they point to the gate. They are afraid to stop in case like the police comes up behind them in an unmarked car. They'd be known like by the police if they are regulars and they don't want to be caught in the Park . . . Sometimes we go to a hotel or the saunas; some do it in the bushes in the Park or drive up the back of the Park or you'll just do it in the car. There's them that just drive around in the car and you'd be blowin' them and then nobody would see you 'cos you'd be bent over BJaying them, you know.

'Most of them would be married with kids. Most of them I know are married. There's this one bloke and I saw him drivin' through the Park one day with a very young fella in the car and I was sayin', "Jaysus, I never saw that young fella up here before", and he parked his car in the car park, he did, and he came up to me and I says, "Who's that in the car with you?" and he says, "That's me son" and I says, "Leave it out." I asked him where he told the young fella he was goin' like, you know, and he said, "For a walk". His son couldn't see where he went because he walked in through the trees to find me. So we did the business while the son was waitin' in the car. He arranged to meet me the followin' week and I says to him, "Get your bleedin' son out of here, you don't want him hangin' 'round here, you'll get blokes tryin' to cruise him if they see him in the car."

'Some of the punters would turn 'round and say "I'm feelin lonely", you know, and "Me wife has me head done in and all like, she's never there when I come home", and all that, you know; they'd be sayin' things like that to you and one fella that I know like his wife died like four year ago and he does say to me, "I feel terrible lonely" like, you know, "Me family and all is there but I feel lonely" and "I do miss me wife" and all this, but why he comes up to me I don't know. I don't know why he just doesn't get a bird like, you know. They do say they enjoy the company and the sex and all. Some of them would be sayin' a woman couldn't blow you for deaths, like, the only way you get a good blow is off another bloke, 'cos, em, they know what it's like and they know what they want and how to give it right, you know.

'They [the punters] could be bisexual like, you know, like a bit of both. Some of them don't know what they want. I was lashed out at by this punter once. I got a wine bottle over the head, I did. I think this fella thought he was gay like and when we were doin' the business he just snapped, sayin', "What the fuck am I doin'", he just snapped on me like, you know, and I got it over the head . . . There'd be some regulars. I might see them once a week. Then you might see someone you haven't seen in ages. They'd be after bein' away or whatever, you know, but you still get a few new faces. When there's football matches on like, you know, you get them up from the country. They'll come up from the country and go into the Park looking for business, you know . . .

'I mainly just do oral sex, you know, like BJs and hand jobs. People have offered me like more money to let them, you know, get up on me. I don't usually do it. I might have to if I'm feelin' sick from the drugs and I need money

40

fast. Some of the punters do bring cream and all to make it less sore. I will ride the punter if he wants but I don't usually let him fuck me. The money can be very good. I remember getting £100 off one fella and £140 off another and you could get more if you wanted, you know. I do fist fuckin' as well. Some of the punters like that. I remember one fella who wanted me to put my whole fist up and I was like sayin', "Leave it out, you lunatic", and I had me gloves on and all like, and he was sayin', "Go on and see if you can get your whole fist up", and I was sayin', "Go away out of that." I had me fingers up and I took them back out and he was sayin', "put it back up, put it back up." You get crazy stuff like that. You couldn't get your whole hand up, for fuck's sake, that's just too much, that is, but you have to do it like, if you want the money, you know, I know it sounds disgustin' and all.

'There'd be only ten or fifteen of us going up there [to the Phoenix Park]. Between the Park, Burgh Quay, the toilets and the saunas, there's like hundreds, even workin' with mobile phones there's hundreds. You go into the men's toilets in town like, you know, and you see "Contact Gerry for a good time" and a mobile number underneath and like, you know, scribbled on the walls and then there's the ads, there's hundreds out there . . .

'I'd like to get into the massage scene 'cos there's good money in it and it's a lot safer. You are not lookin' over your shoulder, you know what I mean, and you are not worried about cars pullin' up beside you like and who it is and whatever, you know.

'Most of the young fellas up there are on gear and that's why they do it like, if it's not drink it's drugs. I'd like to get off the drugs 'cos if I wasn't addicted I wouldn't need to be up there, you know. I used to be takin' coke and Valium as well as heroin but I've got off them and that wasn't easy. I'm still on the heroin. It just makes me feel normal like, you know. It makes me feel like you feel every day, normal. If I haven't got it, I'm goin' around like a bleedin' madman. If I didn't get the money in the Park I'd be thinkin', Jaysus, what am I goin' to do? I'll have to rob somebody, like, you know. I have to fuckin' get it, I just have to, you know.

'I think I'd probably miss the lads in the Park if I left it. I've met some nice genuine people up there, you know, them that would do anythin' for you, and I'm not talkin' sex, just good people, you know . . . I don't know where I see myself in the future, you know [pause]. I either see myself dead or, you know, I don't know. I need to get my life sorted out like, by doin' detox, and maybe then I could get a job and stop goin' to the Park. I don't know how that will happen but maybe, maybe it will . . . maybe I'll get drug treatment but it didn't work before so it probably won't work again, you can't just go off it like that and the programmes they have are shite . . . I'd say the heroin will kill me before I'm thirty.'

3

'Hanging Around'

The Hidden World of Street Prostitution

The public setting of the street prostitute's activity differentiates him from other groups. While escorts and masseurs conduct their business behind closed doors, the street worker often meets his clients in public. Access to the more 'prestigious' forms of prostitution is restricted to the more affluent and better educated. While those involved in street prostitution are the most visible to the public, many of us would be oblivious to its existence. In the social hierarchy of the subculture of male prostitution, the street prostitute occupies the lowest level. It is on the street that most young men begin their involvement in the world's oldest profession. Paradoxically, this is also where they end up when they are too old to continue in off-street prostitution. The street costs nothing and is open for business at any time; there are no dress codes and age barriers to limit admission. For the homeless and penniless – without the facilities to keep a decent appearance and the capital to set up for business – the street offers opportunities which are not to be found elsewhere.

Two men may pass each other on the street; strangers may momentarily share a glance and drop the cues that they are available and interested. Men tour in cars in areas renowned for male prostitution. They identify their 'prey', who signal availability, the contract is agreed and the relationship consummated in any number of places. This is the nature of male street prostitution, which requires no introductions, no prior knowledge, no conversation and no affection. It's an agreement between two men – between prostitute and client – where one seeks to satisfy his sexual desires and the other wishes to make some money. Most passers-by are unaware that this is going on around them. Unlike female prostitutes, male street workers do not dress in a distinctive manner and so the transaction between punter and prostitute regularly goes unnoticed. This is the essence of male street prostitution – anonymous, emotionless sex, for a price.

Those involved in street prostitution generally range in age from fifteen to twenty-five years. Known as 'rent boys', they hang around certain areas such as the Phoenix Park or indeed any park, Burgh Quay, bus and train stations (Connolly, Heuston, Tara Street DART station, Busáras etc.). Many openly solicit and engage in sexual acts in public toilets, such as those on O'Connell Street, toilets in bus and train stations and in shopping centres. Up until recently, the toilets in a city-centre shopping mall were commonly used, but the security guards have now been alerted to the prostitutes' activities. Sometimes, these rent boys may conduct business in clubs, bars or gay saunas.

Many rent boys come from disturbed or dysfunctional family backgrounds. Many feel unwanted and misunderstood, leaving home because of family conflict and the desire for freedom and adventure:

Da left us years ago and after that Mam just lost it . . . she went cuckoo, she did. She was never in the house really and she was always cryin' a lot, loaded to her eyeballs on Valium, she was. She was always in bad humour, always complainin' 'bout not havin' nothin' and callin' me Da names; he was "This fucker" and "That bastard" and all, he was, she'd be callin' him this, tha' and the fuckin' other. I think he went off with another woman, but just left, he did, and she couldn't handle it, she couldn't. Mam was left with us. I think she hated us, she did, and she used always be sayin' that she couldn't wait to get rid of us and that we were useless and all. There was never anythin' to eat, she didn't do shoppin' or anythin'. She was always out on the town. There'd be weeks and she wouldn't come home at all . . . I was only a young fella when Da left, maybe ten or twelve, don't know, but I had to fend for meself, otherwise I'd be dead by now for all she cared. (Robert, rent boy)

Brian remembers his father's reaction when he discovered that his son was homosexual:

He went berserk. I was with this solicitor one evenin' and he had magazines, them gay magazines, you know the ones, and he told me to take them home with me 'cos he didn't want his wife and all seeing them, he didn't want to have them in the car in case she'd get a look at them, all pictures of men's dicks and all they had. I took them home and put them under me bed and went off for the evenin' on the game and when I came back, he was sittin' on a chair just lookin' at me, staring. He had the magazines in his hand and all. He starts callin' me a filthy faggot and all and a bent bastard and things and he says he wasn't havin' any of it in his gaff and all, so I had to leave. I haven't seen much of him since. The day I was leavin' he gave me money and told me to fuck off to me fagotty friends.

The services offered by the rent boys vary, depending on what the client wants and is willing to pay for and what the prostitute is willing to provide. Many rent boys disavow homosexuality and claim to avoid participating in full anal sex, with the exception of those who are homosexually or bisexually identified. Performing sexual acts with men does not necessarily mean that one is homosexual.

I'd never do more than a hand job, maybe a BJ. No way, I wouldn't do full sex. I'm not queer like. I have a girlfriend and all. She doesn't know wha' I'm doing. I'd hate her to find ou' . . . I make enough money without sex, anyhow. (Robert)

I look at it this way: I can have sex with a bloke and get paid for it. I mean if they are willin', I'm able [laughs]. (Brian)

Masturbation and fellatio of or by a client are commonly practised by street prostitutes. Participation in anal sex practices requires higher pay, more time and privacy.

> You can give a BJ anywhere like and it's over quick enough – a pump and a squirt is all it takes. A hand job could be done while sittin' in the car, but if it's anal sex you need to go somewhere. It can take more time like to get the job done – you couldn't really be doin' it in the car like. (Brian)

Sexual acts may take place in the punter's car or home, the bushes, the toilets, the gay saunas or a hotel if the punter is willing to pay.

> Some of the big shots take you to a hotel and some of these are well-known men who do be well into politics and all. It's lucky when that happens and if you get to stay overnight, you can charge a lot of money – 'bout 100 or 150 quid, sometimes more for stayin' the night. He'd go in and book the room while you wait outside and this could be durin' the day and all. There's one punter I do meet and he does give me his mobile phone and when he gets to the room he does phone me with the room number. You follow him in real natural like. If someone stops you, you are fucked 'cos it's not normal for someone like me to be hangin' around. When I do be meetin' him I do be lookin' well so I can get in with' being noticed. If you get to the lift

47

with' being seen, after tha' you have no
problems like. (Robert)

The four rent boys that I interviewed were aged as follows:
Mark – twenty-two, Bob – twenty, Brian – twenty, and
Robert – eighteen. From my observations of the other
boys involved in the rent scene in Dublin, I can conclude
that many are even younger than this.

The punters they do like 'em a bit young and
all so I do often pretend I'm only sixteen or
seventeen and some of 'em really get off on
tha', they do. (Brian)

Usually by his mid- to late twenties, a boy may no longer
be considered attractive and a younger, cuter boy may be
chosen in preference, especially in street prostitution. This
places the boy in a very difficult position as he is unable
to find conventional work because of his street lifestyle.
This may lead to the adoption of other deviant forms of
behaviour such as robbery and drug dealing, which may
bring the former rent boy into trouble with the law.

I don't know wha' I'd be doin', sure I know
nothin' else. Maybe I could get a job on
security or somethin', but there'd be fuck all
money in it. I'd never get enough to get me
gear and anyways I'd be bored out o' me head.
It'd have me head done in just standin' there
with no one to talk to. I'd rather keep doin'
what I'm doin'. (Robert)

Many street prostitutes are abusing drugs – mainly heroin and cocaine. Some rent boys take drugs in order to overcome stress and their sense of revulsion towards sex work. The ready availability of drugs on the street and from some clients augments the degree of vulnerability to substance abuse and works to facilitate addiction. Drugs and alcohol appear to be part of the subculture to which male street prostitutes belong. The types of drugs include heroin, commonly referred to as 'smack' or 'gear'; cannabis, or 'dope'; cocaine, or 'coke'; LSD, or 'acid'; 'speed'; ecstasy;, poppers;, methadone, or 'foy'; and Valium. Many find that after drink and drugs, they are better able to handle clients.

> I'd inject meself with heroin or I'd be smokin'
> it. Tried speed a couple of times. You always
> feel rotten on the way down. Sometimes you'd
> be bleedin' dyin' and you'll do whatever to
> get your hands on more. (Brian).

Street prostitutes may find it difficult to hustle in gay bars, as a result of their physical appearance, but occasionally they gain access and sell their bodies to those willing to pay for it.

> I do often be in there in the pub and some-
> times I do arrange to meet me punters there
> but there's a lot of them who would be afraid
> to be seen in public, you know if they are
> married and they don't be wantin' their wives
> and all to know what they're doin'. (Brian)

Most gay men do not tend to consort with male prostitutes, preferring to be desired for themselves as opposed to paying for emotionless sex. Hence, there is some degree of hostility between the gay and prostitute communities. Homosexuals who use male street prostitutes are usually middle-aged and physically unattractive and this limits the possibility of non-commercial encounters. Often they might seek sexual practices that are not easily obtainable with unpaid partners, such as sadomasochism. The rent boys' regular clients therefore tend to be middle-aged, married men who claim to be heterosexual.

> They're married with kids, in big business.
> Some have loads of money, some of them are
> queer and got married to cover it up. (Robert)

Even though it is now more acceptable to be gay in Irish society than it used to be, many men have not yet come to terms with their homosexuality and, as a result, there is a ready market for male prostitution in this country.

Reasons for involvement in male street prostitution are many and varied (see Chapter 1). Once involved in the rent scene, male prostitutes may identify a number of factors which keep them engaged in it: the access to money and the apparent status that it brings, a sense of belonging to the prostitute community and a sense of power and control in a sexual encounter with a punter, which may differ from previous relationships with adults. The problem may also be exacerbated by low self-esteem and a sense of hopelessness. Prostitution is seen by some as the only alternative to theft, and the main source of income for many rent boys was selling their bodies as opposed to some form of illicit activity.

> If I wasn't on the game I'd be out robbin' and
> attackin' people for money and breakin' into
> houses and cars. (Robert)

In most cases, the financial inducement of male prostitution was enough to overcome any negative factors.

> There's no job that will pay me as good as I
> get in the Park. (Mark, rent boy)

Many were living a hand-to-mouth existence. Hunger and
the need for drugs lead to desperation:

> You either live or you die, that's the choice
> that's in it. I do it to live. I'm too young to
> die. (Robert)

Many male street prostitutes are untrained, unskilled and
poorly educated. As a result, they cannot get well-paid or
interesting jobs. They compare what they earn and the
hours they work in menial jobs to what they earn in
prostitution and it doesn't add up. Many end up quitting
and returning to the streets, where they can earn money
with little effort. For some, the situation seems hopeless:
they cannot sign on because they have no fixed address
and are denied benefits because of their age. Children
under eighteen years in Ireland cannot receive social
welfare, and voluntary absence from an unhappy home
does not entitle a young person to state support. Even if
the boy is eighteen years old, the weekly entitlements are
'so much less than what I can get from two punters up in
the Park in one day'. (Brian, rent boy)

Without a place to live, they find it very difficult to

find and retain employment. It's a catch-22 situation for the adolescent who is detached from his family and living on the streets. In any event, young, single, unemployed males are a low priority for housing in comparison with other groups. As a result, they may turn to such activities as begging, theft and prostitution as their only apparent options in impoverished social circumstances.

There are variations between the rent boys in terms of the amount of money they charge, the location of their work and the kind of services they perform. The amount charged also depends on the rent boy's level of desperation and negotiation skills. Affluent-looking customers will generally be charged higher rates. While many rent boys are reluctant to admit that they engage in anal sex, they generally operate as 'inserters' as opposed to 'insertees'. Denial is more prevalent among those who identify as heterosexual. Robert explained how his pricing mechanism works:

> Well for just a wank, I'd charge £10-£15, more if I think I can get it. For a BJ maybe a tenner more, so 'bout £30-£40 for a wank and a BJ. Yeah, I'd BJ him and he could BJ me if he wanted to, but for me to BJ him I'd ask for more money, another tenner. Some of the fellas have told me that for sex they'd charge over £100, like it's good money and all. Fisting would normally cost 'bout £20 or £30 quid more, dependin' on the punter. Anythin' kinky would cost more again, like for S&M, maybe £50 or even £100. I don't do some of the weird shit that they ask. Some of it would make you puke . . . If you are with

> him for a long time you can ask for more and
> all and if you stay overnight, if I stay over the
> night, I'd ask for £100 and that would only
> be for a wank and a BJ, no sex or nothin'. If
> he's a dead ugly bloke, I'll charge him more.

The amount of money requested depends on each individual rent boy. Lower fees appear to be charged when the prostitute is fellated (receives a blow job) or masturbated or when he performs anal intercourse on the customer. For a customer to penetrate the hustler anally, the price is usually raised. This does not make sense economically, because when the hustler operates in the 'inserter' role and ejaculates, he may not be able to obtain an erection again for some time. This would affect his ability to perform with numerous clients in one night. However, if he adopts the passive role, whereby he is not required to ejaculate, he could presumably perform for longer periods of time. While many rent boys profess their uncompromising heterosexuality, many of them must be sufficiently aroused during sexual encounters to satisfy their clients.

Even though many street prostitutes have a tendency to brag about the high fees they charge, they *can* potentially make substantial amounts of money.

> If I do 'bout five punters in a day, every day
> of the week, I can make a packet. (Robert)

Let's look at this assertion a little more closely. If Robert meets five clients in one day, five days a week, he will 'service' twenty-five clients per week, which is 1,300 per year. If, for example, he charges on average £20 per client (and he would be charging more on some occasions), then Robert could take home £26,000 per year, tax free. However, because of the unpredictably fluctuating nature of the profession, many rent boys do not average five clients per day. Lack of competence in budgeting and handling money, an 'easy come, easy go' outlook on life and substance abuse discourages economy. No home base, long hours spent out of doors and in bars and pubs, alcohol consumption and drug abuse quickly eat up any money that is made.

> Ah there's nights you could be standin' there [Phoenix Park], you could be standin' there for three hours or more and people would drive by not even seein' ya. They'd be there goin' 'bout their business and we'd be lookin' for punters: there might be five or six of us there near the Wellington Monument and we might get nothin' between us for the evenin', and one punter might come along and he might point at one of the other lads, likin' the look of one o' them. There's nothin' you can do and you might be lucky and they might pick you, it depends, really. (Robert)

The street-prostitution subculture has its own specialist 'lingo', which may not be immediately understandable by the outsider. Certain areas of the Phoenix Park are labelled:

> There's a place we do call 'The Meet'. That's were we do pick up the punters durin' the day. The place where we do take the punters in the trees is called 'Fantasy Land', then up

there past the Magazine Hill, we do call the
'S-bends' 'cos the road is all twists and turns.
(Brian)

It is not known how many male prostitutes in Dublin are
controlled by pimps, but this is not thought to be a
common practice. Lack of knowledge about pimps is partly
due to their low visibility. Generally, street prostitutes who
have a pimp do not identify him as such, but as a friend
or boyfriend. This reflects the level of control and fear
which pimps engender. This may well be a significant
and growing problem. In my research, I did not interview
any pimps but I did learn a little bit about them through
the male prostitutes themselves:

These blokes take in the young fellas. They
drive them around in their cars, show them a
good time and give them everythin', until they
agree to work for them. It's not a good idea
'cos they take most of your money out o' ya'
and you're in trouble if you don't hand it over.
They'd beat the shit out of ya'. The Old Bill
[gardaí] don't know and if they did they
wouldn't be bothered anyways. (Brian)

There appears to be a degree of camaraderie among the
clusters of male street prostitutes operating in different
areas throughout the city:

We'd all know each other, we would. Like
there's them that are in the Park, them that
be's on the Quay and you'd always meet the
same ol' faces at the toilets on O'Connell

55

Street or at the stations, you know. I'd know
them all by name and we'd be lookin' out for
each other if somethin' is up. There's a few
of us who goes drinkin' and they'd be them
that I just wouldn't be bothered with. (Bob,
rent boy)

Janus et al. (1984) compared a group of male prostitutes
with a group of boys who were involved in other forms of
street life, namely delinquents, and found that the main
difference in their histories was an absence of coercive
sexual experiences among the 'non-prostitutes'. The
authors concluded that childhood sexual assault serves as
a premature introduction into adult sexuality and teaches
the child to use sex to meet his needs. They see prostitution as a continuation of childhood victimisation. In
my opinion, however, childhood physical and sexual abuse
– although existing in some cases – are not the only
contributors to involvement in male prostitution. Street
prostitution is the embodiment of a number of different
factors that combine to leave the male with no other
alternative.

The majority of male street prostitutes appear to come
from working-class and lower socio-economic backgrounds and have deprived or defective upbringings. Many
of the rent boys have little education and little knowledge
of the state, private or voluntary services that could assist
them. Service providers hoping to help those working in
male street prostitution must consider the complex way
in which involvement became established, so that ap-
propriate strategies can be planned. It is clear that a radical
rethinking of attitudes towards the sex industry and a
change in methods of social control are necessary before

any progress can be made. The message that comes out of my research on male street prostitutes is that, while there are some problem personalities, others would leave the profession if given proper access to jobs and housing – few are pursuing prostitution as a chosen vocation. A knee-jerk reaction of total repression and condemnation of male prostitution is unnecessary and will prove to be counter-productive.

4

'ALL THAT I AM'

BOB'S STORY

Bob is a twenty-year-old homeless boy who has lost contact with his family. His father died when Bob was a baby, and his mother remarried. Bob reported extreme physical and emotional abuse at the hands of his stepfather. This included severe beatings after nights his stepfather had spent on a binge.

He has short, brown hair and is tall and of average build. He has a broad smile but his teeth are rotting. His personality is quite belligerent and he is always defensive. He believes others are out to con him and takes what he can get from people. He feels alone and believes the world is against him. He begrudges those who are better off than he is. He seems incapable of trusting people.

Bob was nervous and distrustful during our first meeting, but on the second occasion he began to relax. At first he was sarcastic and insulting, but as the conversation progressed he realised I was not interested in exposing him and ridiculing his lifestyle. He seemed to welcome the opportunity to talk to someone and, once he had got started, he went into great detail.

Bob doesn't seem to have any close friends. He is emotionless about sex, describing himself as 'definitely straight', and appears to have little regard for his clients. He tends to scorn those who are homosexual and believes he himself is a 'real man'. For him, the lure of 'easy' money is irresistible. He believes those who work are foolish as they have to put in long hours and pay tax. He left home when he was sixteen and has never returned. Bob is an only child and seems to be starved of love and affection.

'I left because of him [his stepfather] and I ended up on the streets. Colette [Bob's mother] used to call the pigs [the gardaí] to come and get me. She didn't want me to be ou' on me own. I used to tell them [the gardaí] that I wanted to stay out all night and that I never wanted to go home again. When they'd be askin' me why, I'd be sayin' nothin' about the batterin's I used to be gettin'. Lookin' back now maybe I should've and he would've gotten wha' he deserved, the bastard. I hope he rots in hell, I do. I hate the fucker.

'He'd come into the house after bein' in the pub for the day and he'd be lookin' for me and all to batter me, he would. He used to punch and kick me till I was sick, he used. I remember one day he hitted me in the mouth and knocked ou' that tooth there, he did. He'd be like an animal when he'd be drunk, callin' me a stupid cunt and all and then callin' Colette a slut and a slag an' all.

'Colette was sick, she was, she had some disease or somethin', she was all weak and all and she was in the bed a lot. She didn't want me to be leavin' and used be worrying 'bout me when tha' bastard be hittin' me and all. She could do nothin' 'bout it, she used just lie there and try and get him to stop . . . No, he usen't be hittin' her. I'd have fuckin' killed him if he did. She went to hospital before I left and I just couldn't be livin' there with him so I left, I did. I don't know how she does be doin' now. I can't be goin' back there, I never do want to clap eyes on that fucker ever and if I do I'll fuckin' kill him . . .

'I left school and everythin', I did, when I left the gaff. I had to look after meself and find places to stay and shit to eat . . . At the start I was stayin' in one of them hostels but 'cos you have to be in at a certain time to get a bed, it didn't suit me when I started on the game. I used to steal back in them days and I didn't want to be beggin' and all but there was times when I had to. I was on the streets 'bout a month or tha' when I met a couple of blokes tha' does be in the Park and they were tellin' me 'bout all the money they do be makin' and all, and they had money like 'cos they were buyin' drink and drugs and everythin'. I remember askin' them how they got their money and when they told me wha' they do be doin', I was thinkin' it was disgustin', you know 'cos I'm straight and all . . . I had no money and no food and they had, so I went with them one of the days and I was thinkin' I could do it a couple of times just to get a bit of money like . . . The first time was in the Park and I got a tenner. I had to just wank the bloke and it took 'bout five minutes and tha' was it, I couldn't believe it. After tha' I became good at it, you know, 'cos the punters liked me, they did. I was the younger of them that was up there at the time. Ya have to be ridin' and all to make money. You can make a lot of money doin' it. I don't be goin' up to the Park anymore 'cos it's too dangerous. Up in the Park one time after Christmas, me and another bloke were walkin' up the road we were and this was around eight o'clock and it was dark and there was these two cars comin' behind us, one was behind the other, and one stopped and I was thinkin' no one will get out of this car 'cos there's another one close behind, so I kept walkin' and next thing, five of them jumped out, they did, and I went leggin' it one way and your man went runnin' the other way like, and I fell down a big drop into a load of thorn bushes like, you know, and they couldn't like see where I was and they caught the other fella. The car tha' was comin' down behind was another gang of blokes, there was 'bout ten of them jumped out and battered the young fella, Paul was his name, tha' I was walkin' up the road with and I was upside-down in the bushes. Afterwards, I went to see how the young fella was and he was all blood and all, he was. They battered him, they did. He walked across the field, he did, in off the road in case they'd come back. I was all covered in cuts 'cos I'd fell into thorn bushes, I looked like I was after gettin' a batterin' as well – me face and me arms was all ripped up. I told the young fella to go to the Old Bill [gardaí] but he wouldn't, not a chance was he goin' . . . I do be on Burgh Quay now . . . you can see more there and it's safer, I do think – more people around and there's more punters. You do have to be careful of the pigs an' all but they do say nothin' really. They do often say to move on and all but that's 'bout it. They don't be arrestin' you or anythin'.

'There does be young fellas being picked up all the time. There's loads of punters. It does depend on the night sometimes. This time of year is grea', they do be everywhere. They do be gettin' real horny when May comes [laughs]. There does be nights I do be standin' there and I do make a lot of money, and if you get a punter who's into havin' a ride with ya, then you could make over a hundred quid. It does depend how long it does take, how long you do be with the punter, you know. A lot does go on along the quay at night. There's them amusements there on Burgh Quay, where the old blokes do play video games and look out for the young blokes who'd be on the game. You'd either go off with them in their cars or go to the toilets on O'Connell Street or in there in Tara Street, they do be doin' the business in there and in Connolly and Busáras there as well. You have to be careful not to be gettin' caugh'.

'When I do be with the punter I do be feelin' nothin'. I do be numb. I do just get it over with and get the money and get the fuck ou' of there. I've no trainin' or nothin' for to be doin' anythin' else. I do it 'cos it's easy money. I can't get money anywhere else.

'I remember me first time on the Quay. I was standin' there all nervous like. I done it a few times in the Park but I was still nervous. I was standin' there and this bloke just comes up to me and he says, "Are you comin' or not", and I went with him. I couldn't believe it. I was just after gettin' there 'bout ten minutes earlier and I have meself a score. I got twenty quid for goin' down on him. It was easy money. I think I done 'bout two more punters that same evenin'. Got 'bout sixty quid.

'I do go there 'bout eleven or twelve at night. Some days there does be nine or ten fellas on the game. Durin' the winter, when it's cold and all, there does be less, five or six. Sometimes there does be only one or two . . . You could be waitin' there till 'bout six in the mornin'. The best times is 'bout twelve or one, when you do get them comin' ou' of the pubs and all, or two or three, when they are leavin' the clubs. If they haven't scored for the night, they might come lookin' for business on the Quays. I do have me regulars as well. There's this bloke who I do be meetin' once a week, Thursdays, and he does drive by and he does always take me, he does, and we do go there to Dollymount beach and do the business. He doesn't be into ridin', he likes to be talkin' and all and likes a BJ and all but that's 'bout it and I do get £30 for 'bout an hour with him. He does be talkin' 'bout not havin' any friends and how he does hate goin' out to the gay clubs and all. He's not very good-lookin' so he does find it hard to be meetin' blokes so he does like to meet me and all.

'They [clients] do be in their forties and fifties. Some o' them is older even. There's one fella I do be meetin' sometimes and I do be thinkin' he's 'bout sixty or seventy. He's got grey hair an' all and does be wearin' a weddin' ring. I do be thinkin' I hope he doesn't die 'cos he does be gettin' all excited and shoutin' and roarin' and all when I do be down on him he does say tha' no one can give a BJ like I do, silly old bastard. Some of them do be terrible ugly and all. Some of them do be bent, but mostly it does be married men who do want to try it out with a bloke.

'The ones in the cars do circle around the Quay, they do, real slow to see is there any business and you do move out to the edge of the path and walk around a little and then they do come back and pull in and you go over and get in, an' they do drive off or else they do pull in 'round the corner there and you go 'round after them. They do pull round the corner in case there does be pigs 'round the place and they do be afraid of gettin' caugh' or being seen by anyone with a rent boy and all. Sometimes hotels, or sometimes we do go to the beach or the saunas or the toilets or else to his gaff. Only one punter ever got rough. Mostly on the Quays them that come are okay. I was in the car with this bloke and he was drivin' ou' to Tallaght and we started doin' the business and next thin' he's batterin' me. I didn't know wha' to be doin' so I legged it ou' of the car and he drove off. I had no top on me or nothin' and it was freezin' and I was stuck ou' in Tallaght. I had to walk back into town. It took me bleedin' ages, it did, and I was fuckin' freezin'. The looks people was givin' me 'cos I had no top on.

'I do go into the toilets durin' the day. You'd go in like and you hang 'round. There might be no one there when you go in. When someone does come in you do go to the sink and dry your hands and do be lookin' at him in the mirror and then you do wait and see if he does look at you. If he does be lookin' at you, you know he's lookin' for business. You go into the toilet then but you don't lock the door. You do make sure he does know that you're on the game – you do smile at him and all. If he's not lookin' for business he does just walk ou' but if he is, chances are he'll come in with ya into the toilet and then you do ask him wha' he wants and that's it . . . I've done ridin' in the toilet, yeah. If someone else comes in and hears noise, they do probably just leave and all . . . the pigs [gardaí] don't come in much, you do be listenin' out for people comin' in and you do be quiet when they do be there. You do be lucky if you meet one or two punters in the toilets in the day. There used to be more there but not any more. There does be all phone numbers on the wall and all and the punters do phone them now instead of doin' it in the toilet. In the shoppin' centres, they [rent boys] do come in with them cordless drills and do drill holes in the walls between the toilets so they can be lookin' in and see who does be in the next one and if they might be lookin' for business. There does be cruisin' goin' on in nearly all the toilets in any of them shoppin' centres and train stations and all.

'The odd time, I do go out to Dun Laoghaire to the pier and there does be punters hangin' around them toilets there on a good day and all. It does be a good spot in the summer. There does be no one there when it does be winter. If it's a really good day, you do have to go somewhere besides the toilets 'cos there does be too many around who's not lookin' for business, they do be in an' ou' of them toilets there like they do have the runs, so we do go off somewhere else.

'I do do a bit of drugs, some heroin and coke, but I'm not a junkie like. I do be doin' it in the evenin' before goin' to the Quays. It does make it easier to be doin' wha' I'm doin' but I don't be needin' it every day. I'm not all fucked up over it but it does be good sometimes. I don't want to be gettin' addicted and all 'cos I do see them lads on the Quays and they do be goin' mad to get money to get more, they do be goin' crazy and all. I'd hate to get gettin' like tha'. Sometimes the punter does have some gear and he'd give you some o' tha' but I do normally prefer to get paid money. I do stay the odd time with punters an' all if they do have a place and all. I do sleep sometimes in the car park at the back of Burgh Quay. I'd make a few pound and then go round the back and sleep in the car park. It does be bleedin' freezin' . . . It's grea' when you do be in a punter's gaff 'cos you can have a shower and somethin' to eat and it's warm and all. There's a bloke who does be on the Quay some nights and if I'm there when he does be goin' home he does let me stay with him . . .

'I don't know, maybe another year or two and then I'll give it up and try and get a job and all and somewhere to stay. I don't know wha' I could be doin', but I don't like wha' I'm doin' and I'd like to get ou' of it but I need the money. When I have enough money I'm goin' to rent a flat of me own and then I might get a job and all. I do like girls and all, sometimes I do be checkin' them ou' when they pass by on Burgh Quay and I do forget I'm supposed to be lookin' ou' for punters. I'd like to be havin' a girlfriend. It does be hard to meet anyone when you do be on the game. I mean, where would she be thinkin' you'd be goin' out all night? I was goin' with this bird once, classy, she was, and she found ou' wha' I was at an' it was all over after tha'. She said she couldn't be goin' out with someone who be's on the game. She said it was disgustin' and all . . . I'd like to be doin' a proper job and all and be gettin' a wages cheque at the end of every week like everyone else an' not have to be goin' to the Quays and all. I think I can do it. I just need to get me flat and move on from there . . . I don't want to be an old bloke and still standin' on Burgh Quay.'

5

'BEHIND CLOSED DOORS'

MALE OFF-STREET PROSTITUTION

In addition to male street prostitution, there are a number of sex workers who operate away from the public eye. These 'off-street' prostitutes are the most prosperous hustlers. They are usually successful by virtue of the fact that they are good-looking, well-built, easygoing, sexually versatile, discreet and maybe even well-endowed. Many of these men are older than those involved in street prostitution, and they are rarely under eighteen. Most identify themselves as homosexuals or bisexuals and are ostensibly comfortable with their sexual identities. They apparently enter the trade with deliberation and out of informed and free choice and can generally make a smooth transition from prostitution to conventional work when they decide to do so. They find prostitution a congenial and profitable activity and a viable source of supplementary income, and they regard it as bringing them into contact with some interesting people and enabling them to have luxurious surroundings and an exciting lifestyle that they would otherwise be unable to afford.

Off-street prostitution is the most lucrative form of

prostitution. Therefore, it is not unusual for the masseur or escort to feel superior to those who operate at street level. In comparison to those who ply their trade on the streets, the off-street workers often enjoy prostitution and have better control over the selection of clients, fees charged and services offered than the street hustler. They also tend to contrast with street prostitutes in social origin, family background, level of education, reasons for involvement, physical appearance, general avoidance of drug and crime dependency and outlook for the future.

Many off-street sex workers come from supportive family backgrounds, choosing to become involved in prostitution as a quick means of earning money and because of their homosexual orientation:

> It gives me an opportunity to enjoy myself and make money.
>
> > (Paul, self-employed masseur)

Many prefer not to refer to what they are doing as prostitution:

> That term applies to those who work the streets. I'm an escort, not a prostitute.
>
> > (Frank, escort)

Unlike the street prostitute, many of the off-street workers are highly ambitious, often using prostitution to tide them over and to attain a better financial standing. Many have the necessary ingredients for happiness: the best in education, family support, money, maturity of purpose and a compatible sexual orientation. This group is less dependent on prostitution for survival, having the basic necessities of life, such as food, shelter and clothing. While their families are often aware of their homosexuality, they are usually ignorant of the fact that their children are involved in prostitution, on any level. Many of the off-street clients have been described as well-to-do business-men, who seek a sexual encounter with another male for whatever reason. Like the street prostitute's clients, many are married, refusing to accept the fact that they may have homosexual tendencies. Off-street prostitutes do not generally report trouble with their clients.

> It's my own place and I feel comfortable here. I know how to defend myself and you can usually tell, anyway, if a client is going to cause hassle over the phone, and if you have any suspicions that they might, you tell them you can't fit them in. As a rule, I don't take clients late at night or if they have been drinking – it's just too risky. After all, you don't know who's out there. (Paul)

For the escort working for an agency, who does not get to vet his own clients, this can be an even greater worry:

> You just don't know who is waiting for you when you do call-outs. They could have someone waiting in the next room to attack you but you have to try not to think like that or you'll drive yourself mad. (Frank)

While many clients are transient, visiting only once, the hustlers often have a list of regulars. In the winter, casual punters are scarce, whereas in the summer, business is inclined to soar. The majority of off-street prostitutes operate under the cloak of an orthodox business. This group includes those who work in escort agencies and massage parlours, self-employed masseurs and those who ply their trade in gay saunas. While it should not be assumed that all those involved in supplying this type of service are male prostitutes, undeniably some of them are. While the gardaí are aware of their existence and of the services they provide, it seems that they have chosen to ignore them (see Chapter 7).

Those involved in the off-street scene have a 'shelf-life', being forced out of the trade when they pass their sell-by date, usually by the age of thirty. (This is particularly so in the case of the escorts working for agencies or masseurs working in parlours). In many instances, the off-street hustlers are part-time and use their earnings to supplement their income from other employment.

The escort is distinguished from other groups primarily by his attachment to an agency, which takes a proportion of his earnings. He offers a full range of sexual services, in the client's or his own home or in a hotel. As he may occasionally be asked to act as a bona fide escort, he is usually better educated, more middle-class and more 'presentable' than the street prostitute. The escort is, therefore, an official employee of the agency, although it is doubtful whether the Revenue Commissioners are aware of this. Fees are fixed, paid by the client to the escort, who gives up to one-third to the agency. The escort is also expected to turn over a certain number of clients per week; failure to do so may lead to the escort being removed from the agency's books. When the escort telephones the agency, his requirements are noted and the fees are quoted.

Overt references to sexual activity are not generally made over the telephone but words such as 'full-body service' give the client an idea as to what is available. Additional payments received by the hustler over and above that agreed with the agency are usually considered to be the hustler's own money.

> We are supposed to hand over a third of everything we earn even if the client decides he wants more later on, but if you get more there's no way you are going to let them know, because they take enough of our money as it is. (Frank)

Typical fees include £50-£70 for a visit to the prostitute's home or £65-£90 for the prostitute to 'call out'. These fees include standard services such as masturbation and fellatio in the passive and active mode. If anal intercourse is required, fees may rise up to £200. The place, time and location of the liaison are agreed with the agency and the escort meets the client without any prior introduction. This is usually followed by a period of small talk, and the payment is made before the sexual encounter.

> The deal is done for you by the agency so you don't have to worry about vetting clients. The only thing – because you have had no previous conversation with the customer, it can be difficult when you first meet them as both of us are on edge. Many are not interested in conversation and it's just down to business. (Frank)

In some cases, the escort agency may also offer a massage service, and the boys are chosen for their youth, attractive physical appearance and willingness to respond sexually to their customers. A penis of generous dimensions is another added bonus.

In order to become an escort, the interested party must attend the agency for interview. Frank described this process:

> I remember the interview well for the job. I'd seen the ad in a magazine and I just phoned it up and an interview was arranged almost immediately. I met this middle-aged guy who runs the agency and he asked me to take off my top first of all. Then he asked me to show him my teeth; he said he couldn't stand bad teeth, 'cos bad teeth leads to bad breath and so on. He checked out my chest, checking for any unpleasant smells, and then he asked me to drop my trousers. I wasn't expecting that part. He had a look at my penis and had himself a quick fondle. He was checking out the size of it and seeing if I would get an erection, and I did. The guy is gay himself. I came all over the place and he told me I'd have to learn how to control it. I was well embarrassed. He asked me was I gay and then asked me what I would be prepared to with the clients. I told him I didn't think it was that kind of business. He told me the money was very good so I decided to give it a go. He said I could leave at any time. I told him I was gay and I got the job there and then.

Frank is a twenty-two-year-old escort who lives at home with his parents. They are oblivious to what he is doing: 'They think I'm working in a takeaway.' He is a university student and says that he decided to get involved in the escort business because he is a homosexual and because he needed the money while attending college. He claims that he will give it up next year when he graduates. He is on call five days a week for an escort agency in Dublin.

Many of the gay saunas in Dublin serve as contact points for male prostitutes and their clients. While many street workers may visit the saunas, some off-street workers regularly arrange to meet clients there. For this reason, the gay saunas are worthy of a mention in this chapter. They are the scene of homosexual promiscuity (money does not change hands) as well as prostitution. On arrival, the man undresses, has a shower and is given a towel to put around his waist. He is then free to roam around in order to find a potential suitor. Many male prostitutes use the saunas to meet clients who are uncomfortable meeting in the hustler's home. Some gay saunas are registered as businesses, under sole traders, at the Company's Registration Office and are operating under the alias of health and leisure clubs. In these saunas, the entrance fee is usually £10-£15, and once inside, the client can avail of sauna, steam-room and shower facilities, private cubicles and what is known as the 'dark room'.

Massage parlours, escort agencies and self-employed masseurs advertise their services in the classified sections of newspapers and magazines. Until recently, such ads were commonly found in *In Dublin* and *Hot Press*, and they can still be seen in *Gay Community News* and *Gay Times*, an English publication which circulates in Ireland and elsewhere. The simple codes in these advertisements are easily broken and the reader is left in no doubt as to the kind of favours on offer. In a recent edition of *Gay Times*, there were eighty-six advertisements under headings for 'escorts', 'masseurs', 'models' etc. These ads, despite their innocent wording, gave broad hints as to the available services. In West and De Villers' book *Male Prostitution: Gay Sex Services in London,* the authors provided details of an advertisement that appeared in *Gay Times* in April 1990:

> Come on! Hot experienced leather man is
> waiting to service you. Tanned, blue eyes, dark
> hair and moustache. Can visit. Tel: —

Looking through the March 1999 issue of *Gay Times*, I came across the very same advert, nine years later. This points to the fact that in some cases, off-street prostitution is a very lucrative and lasting business. Prices are not normally given until the client telephones, and they may vary depending on the time of day or night, how long the hustler is required for and whether any 'special services' are required. Usually, the off-street prostitutes who offer highly erotic services such as sadomasochism etc. are older males who are no longer required for 'routine' sexual activity. The escorts and masseurs appear to be generally in their twenties and are rarely under eighteen years of age.

The number of ads in various publications for these services suggests that business is booming. Among other things, such ads tend to concentrate on the attractive appearance of the hustler's body:

Holistic Massage – Muscular Carl gives best
service in town, in quiet, discreet surroundings. Also call-outs. Ph: —for details.
(*In Dublin*, March 1999)

Steve, Dublin, 22, very good looking, toned,
tanned body, sensual, no attitude. Tantric
service. In/out. Tel: 086 —
(*Gay Times*, March 1999)

Some of the adverts are more blatant than others. It is
difficult to know whether the following advertisement is
for the purposes of prostitution or whether the man
involved is just looking for an unpaid partner:

Bi guy seeks two-way arse and fist fucking
action with guys. Me: slim, well-hung, genuine, can travel & accommodate. Call: —
(*Hot Press*, 9 June 1999)

Masseur and masseuse, relaxing massage for
ladies and gentlemen. Also erotic male escort
(good looking, intelligent, friendly) available
for all. Tel: —
(*Hot Press*, 9 June 1999)

Gentlemen! Enjoy the personal attention of
an experienced male for stimulating and
sensuous massage, Call in/out. Tel: —
(*Hot Press*, 9 June 1999)

Manwatch. Male-to-male muscular masseurs.
Eric 20, Raymond 19, Edward 20. Unhurried

1 hour per session. Discreet. No parking
problems. C.P. available. Hair removal. Video
sales. Also call-outs. Tel: —
(*Hot Press*, 9 June 1999).

These advertisements may also use colours to represent
the kind of sexual services that are available: Some use a
colour-coding system, where blue might denote masturbation and red might denote the availability of full anal
sex or whatever. This would generally be known to the
clients who avail of the service. They might say for
example, "man dressed in boyish blue" or "red-headed
male" or "blue eyes" or something to indicate what's on
offer. (Stephen, ex-masseur).

In Dublin magazine was banned by the Censorship of
Publications Board for six months in August 1999. Before
the ads were banned, there were ten pages devoted to ads
for men and women at the back of the magazine. Although
the decision has since been lifted in the High Court, it
led to the removal of advertisements for massage parlours
and escort agencies in mainstream publications.

A statement from the board shortly afterwards said
the fortnightly publication had been banned because parts
of it were found to be 'indecent and obscene'. Three of
the five members of the board voted in favour of banning
In Dublin under the Censorship of Publications Act 1946.
This followed a complaint by a member of the public in
1998. No specific reasons were given for the ban, but it is
almost certain the controversial advertisements for massage
parlours, escort agencies, adult videos and saucy telephone
conversations were to blame. The ban prevented the sale
or distribution of *In Dublin* on or after 10 August. The
magazine's publisher, Mike Hogan, appealed the decision

to the Censorship of Publications Appeal Board. While books and magazines have frequently been banned in the past, most of them were explicitly pornographic. There was a mixed reaction to the Board's decision and many believed the decision was too harsh.

Following Mr Hogan's appeal, the ban was subsequently lifted on the grounds that all ads promoting sexual favours had been removed. Shortly afterwards, a new, cleaner *In Dublin* returned to our shelves. The Personals section of the new *In Dublin* has been sanitised and all the ads for massage parlours and escort agencies have been removed. Similarly, *Hot Press* has removed such ads, obviously fearing the wrath of the Censorship Board. However, *Hot Press* still carries ads selling adult videos and promoting fetish activity.

While the ads have been removed from the aforementioned publications, it is doubtful whether this will go any way towards curbing the male sex industry in Ireland. There are always plenty more publications to choose ads from.

*

Stephen was working for a massage parlour in Dublin until five years ago, when, at the age of twenty-eight, he was told that he was no longer required. Stephen explained how a massage parlour located close to the city centre operated:

> The client goes in and pays a fee at the desk. It was £25 then; I think it has gone up to about £30 these days. I wouldn't be sure; that's for a basic massage. There is usually a bouncer

type at the outer desk to screen customers. These places operate as massage and health clubs and you'll see keep-fit posters and all on the walls. There's a sauna and steam room there and I think they've gotten a jacuzzi since I left. The client comes in and he's given some photos to look at of the boys and he chooses the masseur he wants from these. This one had about six or seven guys working in it when I was there. We were all in our twenties and no one was kept on after thirty. When I left I was twenty-eight and that's not over the hill but they felt I was too old. The clients tend to prefer them younger and fitter than I am. Anyway the customer chooses the one he wants and he has a shower and puts on a towel around his waist and he's shown into a cubicle, where the masseur is waiting naked for him. He's instructed to lie down on the massage table. So, the masseur will generally start off with a normal massage and he'll stand real close to the client, pressing against him, and will remove the towel, caressing his arse or whatever. If no further money changes hands, this is as far as it goes. If the client asks for more, like hand relief or a blow job, this will cost him. It would be another £10 for hand relief, £15 for mutual masturbation, maybe £20 for a blow job and it could be anything from £100 to £200 for two-way anal intercourse. I don't know exactly what the prices are now. I'm sure they've gone up as everything else seems to have . . . There are

peepholes all over the place so the management can keep an eye on the masseur and
the client to make sure there is no trouble . . .
Don't get me wrong – not every single person
that comes in wants sex, some would just have
a massage and maybe a chat. These places
are absolutely discreet: no signs up about what
is on offer; everything is done verbally and
there's little trace that any other activity is
going on. There is no sign of anything illegal.
The owners know exactly what they are at
and they know how to dodge the law. If these
places are raided, the manager will just deny
that he knew any of it was going on. He'll
say he thought he was running a massage
parlour – no funny business. There are more
of these places around . . . Most of the owners
know one another. It's like one big family. A
lot of businessmen come in. They see this as
a way of relaxing on their lunch break or after
a long day's work.

Stephen is now working as a mechanic and claims that he
found the shift from prostitution to conventional work
trouble-free, although the hours are longer and the pay is
substantially less. He has now formed a steady relationship
with another male – something he found impossible to
do while working as a prostitute. His present partner is
unaware that he spent six years working as a prostitute,
from the age of twenty-two to twenty-eight.

I just couldn't tell him, I don't know how he'd
handle it. I'm afraid to lose him.

Even though masseurs may be tied to an agency operating under the guise of a massage parlour, it appears that most are self-employed, providing a full range of sexual services. While the escort is rarely called upon to escort, the masseur is usually required to practise the trade of his title. This is often used to relax the client prior to sex. It is said to be rare that clients settle for only a massage, but it has been known to happen on occasion. The self-employed masseur organises his own advertisements, thereby freeing himself from the control of an agency. Earnings become tax-free, but the masseur may also have to deal with direct exposure to hoax calls, lacking the protection that an agency can provide. The contract is formed directly between the client and the prostitute over the telephone. Negotiation over the type of service provided and the price has a flexibility that is absent in the case of the escort. However, the freelance masseur usually adopts agency rates.

Paul described how the self-employed masseur operates what can be a very lucrative business:

> I have one room in the house for massage. I
> bought a special bed. You need it 'cos it's at
> the right height to the body to provide a
> proper service . . . The client phones and you
> generally try and suss him out over the phone
> to see if he's all right. You arrange a time and
> give him the area. I usually don't give out the
> full address until the morning of the appoint-
> ment. I get them to phone again on the
> morning when they get to the general area.
> There is a phone box that I direct them to

and tell them to phone me when they get there. That makes it easier for me to determine whether or not they are coming. If they don't phone by the time I say, I take it they are not coming. When they get to the house, I offer them a light drink, maybe a beer if it's the evening, and we have usually a short conversation, depending on the client. I have a good personality so many of my regulars enjoy chatting to me. Then we go into the massage room, where I conduct a very sensual massage and whatever else the client is willing to pay for. I will do anything except anal sex because I prefer to keep that for my non-paying partners. I charge £50 for a massage and anything extra is extra. I charge heavy sums for any erotic activity. For an hour of S&M, I could charge up to £100 or £150.

Paul is a forty-five-year-old bisexual, self-employed masseur, living in a small but comfortable house on the north side of Dublin which he runs as a B&B for regular clients.

Many off-street prostitutes fear being raided by the gardaí as their activities could quite easily be construed as brothel-keeping. The masseur, escort and owners would be eligible for imprisonment if such a garda raid was successful (see Chapter 7).

With the decriminalisation of male homosexuality in 1993, instead of withering away – as many people expected – the availability of male prostitutes increased because advertising in the gay press was capable of reaching a wider audience. It is difficult to estimate the numbers of off-street prostitutes in operation, but by scanning through the classified sections of gay magazines and some mainstream publications, I have reason to believe that there are hundreds plying their trade in Dublin and even nationwide.

The use of the telephone system for the transmission of obscenities is illegal, but this has not prevented the proliferation of 'chat lines' and other services of a quasi-sexual nature, which enable callers to partake in 'saucy' conversations with strangers. Numerous advertisements for such services can be seen in *Hot Press*, *In Dublin*, *Gay Times* etc. The fact that so many of these ads exist points to the widespread demand for sexual contact which is not being met through ordinary social channels. This is a form of 'telephone prostitution'.

Successful male off-street prostitutes who have a consistent and satisfied clientele may have little in common with the sad characters seen on the streets. Many off-street prostitutes are earning considerable sums of money. In a typical week, I estimate that a self-employed masseur could have an average of three clients per day, five days a week (some masseurs work seven days), at £60 per client (many charge more, depending on the service provided). In the average year, therefore, the prostitute would 'service' 780 clients, earning a startling £46,800 tax-free! The busiest times of the day are lunchtime and from 5 pm onwards, while the most productive time of the year is during the summer.

The typical image of the male prostitute as a problem person derives from undue concentration on those involved at street level. There is a constant source of bias in studies of this kind. Rent boys working in public places comprise only a small percentage of the male sex industry. Workers of vastly different backgrounds and characters are employed in a variety of off-street services, some of which are organised into large and lucrative business enterprises. In any study of male prostitution in Irish society, off-street prostitutes are as important as those working on the street in order to provide an understanding of its functioning and dynamics.

6

'INVISIBLE'

DAVID'S STORY

David lives in a plush two-bedroom apartment in Dublin's city centre. He is a twenty-four-year-old homosexual. He has loving and supportive parents and was one of two children. His sister was tragically killed in a motor accident when David was seven years old. His mother, he says, has never fully come to terms with the death of his sister. His parents are aware of his homosexuality but have no idea of that he is a prostitute. He has been working for over a year as a male prostitute, in the guise of a masseur. He is strikingly handsome and well-built, with short, black hair, brown eyes and tanned skin. His manner is friendly and easygoing. He has a regular clientele and also caters for newcomers.

He is always well-dressed and is very concerned about his image. He spends a lot of money on clothes and says he does well because of his good looks and his personality. He was polite and very welcoming when I first visited his apartment. At first, he did not seem willing to admit to prostitution but after I assured him of complete confidentiality, he spoke openly about his involvement. He is not ashamed of what he is doing and sees it as a lucrative means of earning money. He is adamant he could never maintain a similar standard of living through conventional work.

David is originally from the south of Ireland and attended the University of Limerick before coming to Dublin to work part-time from 9 am to 1 pm every day. For the remainder of the day, David operates as a 'masseur' and intends to continue in his dual role for the next year, claiming that economic gain is his primary motivation:

'I got involved initially for the money. When I left university I went backpacking. I backpacked through Asia and ended up in Australia and was working in Sydney as a waiter. Most of the guys in the restaurant were gay and were working for an escort agency, so I said I would give it a try. You see, in Australia it is quite legal, so it wasn't really a problem there. I came back to Ireland with a lot of money, not because of the waitering but because I was working as an escort. When I got home, I decided to set up my own massage service and see if I could get business. I placed an ad in *Hot Press*, *Gay Community News* and *Gay Times*. Shortly after I set up, I started getting calls and the business started to grow.

'You can get *Gay Community News* in a lot of news-agents but there is one along the quays and you can get it there for certain. You can also go to Outhouse, where *Gay Community News* is published, and there is a coffee shop there as well and that's where I go to get my condoms and stuff because they are free. Outhouse is there on South William Street . . .

'You have to advertise to get business. I found that

after a while if you stop advertising you will lose customers, because a lot of them don't even want to keep my number because they are scared in case someone will find out. So you have to keep advertising just so they can get your number when they need it. It is strange really – people are so much in the closet that they won't even keep a number in their diary or anything like that. The *Gay Times* is good – no other gay Irish guy advertises in it. I mean, the price might put some of them off – it's £65 a month, so that would put people off, and it's quite good 'cos you can get Americans as well and they just love the Irish guys. They love the accent and all that kind of rubbish and they are great because they tip quite well, I mean one guy gave me £300 and I didn't do anything more than massage and a blow job. Some of them take you out to dinner and stuff but I don't enjoy that 'cos if you don't enjoy their company, you won't enjoy the food. That happens rarely. It probably happens more among the females and in other countries, I don't know, but here it's rare.

'Some of the ads are quite explicit. Some openly mention fist-fucking and anal sex and there is no massage on offer there, I can tell you. When I went to place my ad I was told I could only advertise as a masseur and I did. Maybe if you've been advertising with them for a while, they let you change the wording. I don't know. It's not legal to advertise very explicitly and yet they seem to get away with it.

'Well, I do a full body-to-body hot-oil massage, which is a full tantric massage, very like a Thai massage. I did a Thai course when I was backpacking in Asia. I do a full body-to-body massage and we are both naked. I massage the full body. I massage the back, the legs, the feet, the chest, their penis if they wish. Some people want a massage, some people don't. A lot of married guys, all they want to do is be able to touch and feel another guy. That's basically what I do and really what they want at the end of the day is for me to get an erection – this is their big thing, because a lot of them are closet gays. About 75 per cent of the guys coming to me would be married. They are generally confused about their sexuality. This generation is changing and it is becoming easier to be gay, but in the last generation, everyone got married . . . Many of them are really homosexual and at the end of the day most gay guys can perform with a girl. Even I have been with some girls. I know from talking to the gay guys that come to me. I have a lot of regulars whose sex lives with their wives have failed to satisfy them and I know there are a lot of frustrated women out there. So they have a massage and they can touch me up as much as they like. Kissing – just barely touching the lips, nothing more, no deep kissing; they can have hand-relief and a blow job if they wish but this will cost them £70 with a massage . . . I don't do full sex – I say that on the phone so no one is in any doubt . . . I do call-outs only to hotels. I won't go to someone's home because it's just too dangerous.

'I have been doing this now for over a year, so [I have] good regulars – I would have about thirty – that would be people I have seen about ten or fifteen times, at this stage. There are business people from England because I have an ad in the *Gay Times* as well – that's an English magazine – and they call me a few times a year when they are on business in Dublin. I get a lot of people from the countryside, farmers up from the countryside. You wouldn't believe they could possibly be gay or bisexual –

you know, the real rough farmer types – it opens your eyes like. I can assure you that the camp queens you see are the minority of gay people – they are the real minority. Most people are just normal people.

'I've been lucky so far. I try and find out as much as I can about someone in conversation over the phone and I probably discriminate because anyone with a dodgy accent, I tell them that I'm not working. You get a lot of perverts ringing up, like you get some guys ringing up and they want you to talk dirty to them and then there are those who are probably having a wank while you tell them what you do, but you can generally tell the weirdos and you just refuse to meet them, you know.

'There's this big farmer type who lives alone somewhere in the midlands who comes to see me. He seems to be a successful farmer but works very hard at it. He has no social life and no friends, from what I can make out. He's a bad conversationalist and as far as I can see he finds his homosexuality repulsive. His father – he's dead now – would have been one of those real macho types, from what I can gather, and he was never with a man till his mother died two years ago. He comes here almost every week when he might have business near Dublin, he says. He's a very lonely man and I do feel sorry for him. His manners are appalling and his hygiene isn't the best either, but as long as he agrees to have a shower when he arrives I don't mind. Sometimes I think it's the only shower he has for the week [laughs]. He loves the massage and likes me to play with his penis. He always insists on giving me a blow job. I think he thinks I enjoy it or something, but he pays well and always throws me extra money . . .

'The ages surprised me actually. I expected it to be about forty-five to sixty but it's not – anything from eighteen to sixty and a lot more young people than you would imagine. Young people who are living at home with their parents who are too scared to go to gay clubs or bars. Nearly all of them are in the closet. I'd say very few of them would be 'out', so to speak.

'I think I am good at what I do. I'm quite friendly and good-looking and that helps and I can always get an erection, which is really what they want, so physically I'm very much in there with them. Emotionally, obviously not – it does nothing for me. There are a couple of people who I get on well with, but it's more talking than anything else because they tell me about their lives so I do get to know them and stuff. I would say I'm as close to guys as anyone else would be . . . I'm a sensual person but I can totally switch off to work and pleasure. I'm good at that. They don't realise that most of the time, and that's for the best. They think because I'm really nice that I really like them. A lot of them want to believe that I really like them a lot of the time. A lot of them are very lonely people but again a lot of them are not lonely but are very busy people and drop in for an hour at lunchtime and they are off again.

'I work depending on my mood, to be honest with you. Well, last week, which was a very average week, I worked five days, starting after I came home from work, and I saw fifteen people in five days, which was averaging about three per day. Some paid £50, some £70; some paid more than that because they just give you tips. One guy gave me £100 last week, so I did well. If I work five to six days, I will never make less than £700 or £800. I've often made more than that. I'm doing it for the money. Why else would I do it? I can get a partner for nothing myself any day of the week for satisfaction, so that's definitely not the reason. I turn on my phone about two. I come home and have a shower, have some lunch and stuff. It varies, it really varies, but I will not work after eleven at night even during the weekend. I wouldn't; again it's for safety reasons, and with people having a few drinks it could turn messy or ugly, but I work basically from three to eleven. It can be busy at any time. There may be days that I might meet three people between three and seven, it just varies. Even when I come in and turn on the phone I have lots of messages already. I think there is even a bit of a demand for lunchtime trade but I would say that three to nine is a good time. Most days are busy – there are no real quiet days.

'I'm originally from the south of Ireland and my parents are still living there. They know I'm gay, obviously, but they have no idea that I work as a masseur. As far as they are concerned I work in Dublin part-time and then I work as a waiter in the evenings. They'd be shocked; shocked, disappointed, gutted and ashamed. Two of my gay friends know, but they are really liberal anyway, both of them would have touched on it as well; two other gay friends in Dublin don't know. This is one of the downsides to the job – you have to tell a lot of lies. I tell people I have a two-bedroom apartment, and when anyone comes to stay I have the other bedroom locked. As far as anyone is concerned I'm renting the apartment from a guy who is gone off travelling and he keeps his room for storage. This is a downside to what I'm doing – the fact that I have to lie. Your whole life is a lie in a sense, except for the few people that know what I do; you have to keep to the same story all the time.

'Obviously, it's not legal, is it, but nobody really knows this is going on, even with advertising. You are supposed to be a masseur, which is fine for me because I'm qualified – well, semi-qualified. I know what I am doing. Some of them advertise as a masseur and they haven't a clue what they are doing. They are only advertising as a masseur because it's legal. Obviously, when I started up in Dublin, I didn't know whether I would get raided or not but so far nothing has happened. I didn't know whether the police would come round and arrest me but they haven't. As far as I can see, with the male side anyway, as long as you are off the streets, I don't really think they care. I'm sure if they got complaints they might do something . . . The policemen did come around here a couple of weeks ago. I was totally unlucky, really unlucky, for a totally different reason. The previous tenant here, they were checking out a stolen credit card and chequebook so they banged on my door at 8 am. I answered the door and five policemen were standing there. I thought, what am I going to do, they are on to me. I was really unlucky 'cos they were there for a different reason but they searched the whole place and they searched the spare room and they asked me what I did and I said sports massages, but I mean they could see condoms and stuff there, but that was two weeks ago and nothing happened, so obviously they don't care . . .

'I think there will always be a demand for this type of service because there will always be old guys or ugly guys or shy guys or guys with tiny dicks. For all those reasons, guys will come to me, so I think there will always be a demand . . . The important thing is to do other things and not just massage. At least I'm working as well because it gives me another focus. If I was just doing massage, I would go brain-dead, you would like. It's also important to only do it for a short time. As the masseur gets older, he will be less attractive. I think the gay scene is worse for depending on body beautiful and youth, more so than the straight scene. I mean, if you look at, say, magazines for women, there will be pictures of say, George Clooney and the women think he is gorgeous, whereas a gay guy might look at Nicky Tilsley from Coronation Street, that is the difference, so definitely the gay scene is about being beautiful, which is sad . . .

'I'll do this for about another year and then I might start working full-time and maybe do some sports massage in the evenings. I'm doing a course at the moment one day a week and I would very much like to get into it. I might maybe continue to meet regulars as well – those who have my number – but I intend to stop advertising in another year or so; well, that's the plan so far, anyway.'

7

'SEXPLOITATION'

THE LEGAL CONTEXT
OF MALE PROSTITUTION

Since 1993, sexual contact between two men is no longer a criminal offence, provided that it takes place in private and between two consenting adults. The age of consent is seventeen years in the Republic of Ireland and eighteen years in Northern Ireland. After the legislation was passed, it was believed that the level of male prostitution would be severely affected. It was felt that, with the opening up of the gay scene, clients would no longer need to avail of prostitutes. This, however, does not appear to have transpired. It seems that as long as the male sex industry is in existence, it will never lack regular custom.

Prostitution by both males and females is an offence in many countries, but surprisingly, this is not the case in Ireland and England, although its practice is controlled by the Criminal Law (Sexual Offences) Act of 1993. According to this act, it is not the prostitution itself which is illegal but 'soliciting' and 'loitering' for the purposes of prostitution, living off immoral earnings and other related offences. In reality, this makes the practice of prostitution more difficult, but not impossible. These laws attempt to regulate prostitution in this country. Raymond Byrne, barrister-at-law, explains that 'Really, in a sense, it is the public aspect of it [prostitution] which is illegal. If it is done in private, it is not illegal, but if it is organised, then it's a brothel, and that's prohibited.'

The current legislation in Ireland covering male prostitution is the Criminal Law (Sexual Offences) Act of 1993. Section 7 of the act states that 'A person who solicits or importunes another person or other persons for the purposes of prostitution shall be guilty of an offence – '.

I spoke to two gardaí who have considerable experience with the problem of male prostitution – in fact, they come into contact with male prostitutes on a daily basis. According to one of the gardaí (Garda 1):

> Male prostitutes and clients can be charged
> under the Sexual Offences Act of 1993 if they
> are believed to be engaged in male prosti-
> tution. You would have to have sufficient
> belief that the transaction has taken place. If
> a statement was being volunteered by either
> party, that would be more than enough
> evidence. The first offence carries a fine of
> £250 and the subsequent offence carries a fine
> of £500 and/or three months in prison. This
> is according to Section 7 of the act.

While the primary purpose of the act was to decriminalise male homosexuality to comply with a European Court ruling on the matter, secondary clauses refer to prosti-tution. No distinction is made in the act between male and female, adult or child. According to Section 2 of the act, a person is guilty of 'soliciting' and 'importuning' for the purposes of prostitution if that person:

- offers his or her services as a prostitute to another person
- solicits or importunes another person for the purposes of obtaining that other person's services as a prostitute
- solicits or importunes another person on behalf of a person for the purposes of prostitution.

The offence applies to soliciting or importuning by a prostitute, the client or a third party, whether male or female. There is also a section in the act relating to 'loitering for the purposes of prostitution'. According to Section 8, 'A member of the Garda Síochána who has reason to suspect that a person is loitering in a street or public place in order to solicit or importune another person or other persons for the purposes of prostitution may direct that person to leave immediately that street or public place.'

Thus, under this section, the gardaí can order a person to leave a public place if they suspect that they are there for the purpose of prostitution. An offence is committed when the person fails to comply with the garda caution. This section also includes loitering in a motor vehicle, in the Phoenix Park or on Burgh Quay, for example, and can apply to the prostitutes or their clients. Garda 2 says:

> You see them hanging around the Park and you ask them to move on. If you asked them to move on and you came back later and they were still there, you could arrest them the

second time, because you have already asked them to leave the first time. You'd warn them and say, 'If I come back and you are still here, you will be arrested and that's it, now get out of here and get out of the Park.' That is what I would say to him and by telling them to move on you mean get out of the Park, not just to move away from the spot they are in to another location. Moving them down the road just isn't enough.

Masseurs and escort-agency workers and owners can also face imprisonment on charges of brothel-keeping or profiting from the earnings of prostitution (Sections 9, 10 and 11 of the Sexual Offences Act of 1993) or possibly for tax evasion. Because such acts occur in private and under the guise of a legitimate business, many masseurs and escort-agency workers have so far avoided any trouble with the law. Stephen, an ex-massage parlour employee, says, 'No, as far as I know it was never raided, I mean the gardaí don't seem too worried about such operations, they adopt the attitude of let them be and everyone is happy.'

When they freely advertise, you can keep a certain check and know what is going on and keep a running brief on who is engaged, how much of it is going on and make sure it is relatively crime-free, that there is no rape or larceny going on. I wouldn't say that it's a casual approach. I would say that the gardaí have and do take an interest. It's a problem which is hard to cap fully and, as I say, when it is underground it tends to have a lot of

The Wellington Monument in Phoenix Park:
A well-known hangout for rent boys after dark. Clients often
approach these railings looking for rent boys.

Bench beside Magazine Hill:
This bench is used by Mark and some other prostitutes to meet
clients who know where to find them.

Polo grounds beside Áras an Uachtaráin:
After meeting with the rent boys, clients in cars often park in this
area late at night.

Toilets and changing rooms in Phoenix Park:
A meeting point for clients and rent boys. Security has become a lot
tighter in this area in recent times.

Magazine Hill:
During the day in the summer months, clients park
their cars in this area when they go on foot to meet the
rent boys.

Burgh Quay:
Rent boys hang around this general area and clients drive by slowly before stopping to pick them up. This usually happens late at night.

Toilets on O'Connell Street:
These are often used by rent boys and clients. Walls inside are often used as a means of exchanging phone numbers.

> things running hand in hand with it which
> would be more serious than prostitution itself.
> (Garda 2)

Off-street prostitution by its nature is quite discreet and is unlikely to come to the attention of residents or the authorities. This invisibility tends to diminish police interest in it. If the behaviour is out of the public eye and is not accompanied by other crimes, the gardaí may choose not to interfere. Off-street prostitutes break the law just as much as the street prostitutes and are readily traceable through their advertisements. The difficulty in gathering evidence, however, may act as a deterrent:

> The kind of undercover work that would be needed in the parlours and agencies is not being done enough. It's so obvious that they are ignoring the problem; that's basically what it is, they are ignoring the problem and are pretending that it is not there. You could get a search warrant and go into these places. A garda sergeant can go to a judge and can fill in what is called 'an information', stating the premises he wants to search, what he hopes to find there, his reasons for raiding it and that the information he is looking for will be there, and you can force your way in if you have a search warrant. (Garda 1)

Section 9 of the Sexual Offences Act deals with the organisation of prostitution and could be enforced in relation to massage parlours and escort agencies. It refers to those who control and direct the activities of prostitutes, i.e. pimps and anyone who coerces another person to be a prostitute. The penalties are up to £10,000 or up to five years in prison, where the conviction is on indictment (this is a more serious offence). For example, if the case is heard in the District Court, the individual is liable to a fine of up to £1,000 or imprisonment for a period of up to six months. However, if the case is heard in the Circuit Court, the individual may have to pay up to £10,000 or serve five years in prison.

Section 10 refers to a person who 'lives in whole or in part on the earnings of the prostitution of another person' or who aids and abets prostitution. If a person is found guilty of one of these offences, they are liable to 'a fine not exceeding £1,000 or to imprisonment for a term not exceeding six months or to both'. Section 10(3) can be enforced if a member of the Garda Síochána, not below the rank of Sergeant, applies to the District Court for a search warrant for a premises where he suspects it is being used for the purposes of prostitution and that the person living in or frequenting the premises is living in whole or in part on the earnings of prostitution. The gardaí can then enter the premises and arrest the people involved. Section 11 deals with brothel-keeping, which is an illegal activity. Those liable for prosecution include the landlord, the tenant or occupier who knowingly allow the premises to be used for the purposes of prostitution, and any person who manages or keeps a brothel. On conviction, the fines imposed are the same as for an offence under Section 9.

Raymond Byrne (barrister-at-law) adds, 'Sexual activity on these premises would come under brothel-keeping if organised. The gardaí could get a search warrant and search these premises if they have a reasonable basis to assume that the place is operating as a brothel. It's a question of being able to prove that sexual activity is taking place. The offence is difficult to prove. It depends on what the gardaí see as evidence.'

Section 13 of the Sexual Offences Act refers to the powers of arrest of the Garda Síochána. If the garda suspects that a person is soliciting for the purposes of prostitution or has committed gross indecency with a male under the legal age of consent or with a mentally impaired person, then he can arrest that person without a warrant. An offence is committed when the person fails to comply with a direction from a garda and includes a maximum fine of £500.

The laws in relation to prostitution will never force all of those involved in the profession, whether male or female, to cease their activities. One purpose they appear to serve is to keep prostitution hidden from public view. Law-enforcement strategies have failed to eradicate prostitution because clients will always be willing to engage in illicit sex, and garda interference tends to push the practice out of sight, rather than out of existence:

> Arresting the clients or the prostitutes is not the answer. This will only move the problem. It will not get rid of it, it will only move it elsewhere. You are moving it to another area and maybe even to another area of the Park [Phoenix Park]. This will make it more difficult to keep an eye on them. (Garda 2)

The legalisation of prostitution could enable those involved to work with protection from the gardaí and the legal system, making their work less dangerous. The gardaí I spoke to, however, did not agree with this option:

I don't think legalising it is the answer. There will always be people who will use the Park and they tend to be people who don't want to be in the public eye and wish to avoid the public for a lot of reasons, I think mainly because they are married or have girlfriends or something similar and so are loath to let it come out that they are gay. (Garda 1)

I wouldn't agree with legalising it. I mean, to be honest with you, I don't have the answer to this problem, but I don't think it's totally a garda problem, and that's like passing the buck, but I don't think it is totally a criminal problem, it's a social problem as well and legalising it won't solve the problem.

(Garda 2)

The level of male prostitution is regulated in Phoenix Park by means of a garda patrol, which has been in operation in there for the past year and a half:

I prefer to just make myself aware of who is in the car and I would ask them who they are and what the nature of their business is. I have no real power to get a response from them and if they tell me they are just driving through, then I have to accept that.

(Garda 2)

The only reason we use the marked car is to show them that there is a police presence and that we are there, to show the clients that we are there and to try and get rid of them. That's what we are working at – we are working at getting rid of the clients. I would have some sympathy for the prostitutes, but I wouldn't have any for the clients. (Garda 1)

The punitive approach of the Irish legal system in relation to male prostitution is not an adequate solution. Where a fine is imposed, often the way it is paid is by returning to prostitution. It can become a vicious circle for the male street prostitute who is arrested:

I've never arrested any of the male prostitutes that I see in the Park [Phoenix Park], and they have come to my attention because I see them up there all the time, but no, I've never arrested them. When I see them out at night I tell them to move on, then they are back the next day, you know. I don't see the point in arresting the rent boys because they are just going to move on somewhere else and carry on, you know. We have never been given instructions and we know the law and all that, but you are usually given instructions like 'They are all to be arrested' or something like that, but such an instruction has never been given to us. So it's a collating system we use, whereby you collate names into a book and therefore, you know, if something happens in the Park that night, who was there. (Garda 1)

The male prostitutes themselves are not overly concerned about punitive measures:

> These fellas wake up in the morning and all they can think of is where they are going to get their next fix. They don't care if they get arrested. His family would have an idea what he is doing or else he has lost contact with them and any friends he has left are probably on the game with him, so he doesn't care about being arrested. (Garda 1)

The gardaí also become frustrated and disillusioned as they watch the male prostitutes falling through the system. The latter rarely receive the maximum sentence or pay the fines:

> The garda on the street has no incentive to be arresting the male prostitutes, to be bringing them in and seeing them walk out of court with a fine that he is never going to pay. You know that you are going to be following him to pay for it the next year or so, and if he does pay it, it's because he went back into prostitution or because he robbed someone to get the money. (Garda 1)

The level of intervention and punishment in Ireland is relatively less for prostitution than it is for some other kinds of criminal behaviour. The gardaí appear to take a relaxed approach towards male prostitution, both on and off the street, and as a result many male prostitutes do not feel threatened by the gardaí:

Sure I know them all [the gardaí], at this stage. They often stop me on their way by, you know, and they says like, 'Now you get out of the car', to me and then they take your man's name and address that I was with like. We'd see the police comin' like, you know, and I'd turn round to the punter and say, 'Well if they are goin' to stop us and like they tell me to go one way and you to go the other, if you wanna meet me, I'll meet you down at the pub on Islandbridge', and the police will come along and we'd be just sittin' there like and they says, 'What are yiz doin'?' and I'd say, 'Ah we're just yappin'', but they'll turn around to the punter and say, 'You know that he's a rent boy?' and your man will turn round and say, 'What? He's no bleedin' rent boy', and they'll say, 'We know him, like, you know,' and your man will say, 'ah no, I'm a good friend of his father', and I'll be sayin' to the other guard, 'Jaysus, don't be tellin' him wha' I do be doin', you know, but they'd be well wise, they do know well what does be goin' on. (Mark, rent boy)

Another major difficulty in policing prostitution is the degree of emphasis placed on it by garda authorities themselves. It is often not considered a priority, even in areas like the Phoenix Park where it is prevalent, unless there are particularly vociferous complaints by the general public:

We have been getting a lot of phone calls recently, around six and seven o'clock in the evening from people up around the Furry Glen walking their dogs and seeing two or three fellas in the bushes together . . . I don't think that curbing male prostitution with regard to the specific act of prostitution would be high on our list of priorities, but as I said, a lot of crime happens with male prostitution and there have been many robberies of the customers and this would be a concern and keeping tabs on the crime; and many of the boys involved in male prostitution in the Park would have a drugs problem, mainly heroin, and they will do anything to get money for drugs. That means assaulting and robbing clients if they have to. At least in the Phoenix Park, we know the ones with the potential and we would have possible suspects every time, if a certain type of crime happens in the Park. (Garda 2)

The inability of the gardaí to tackle the problem of male prostitution is exacerbated by lack of proof:

They can't prove nothin', you know, they have to, the only way they can arrest ya by law is that they have to see the money you know changin' hands, like they'd nearly have to catch you doin' the business. If they come along like and I'm in the car in the Park with a bloke and we were doin' the business and they caught us in the act, there isn't still a lot

they can do but tell us to get out of the fuckin'
Park or bring us down to the station and like
fuckin' try and get it ou' of the punter that
I'm a rent boy and tha' he's payin' me and all
or get me to say tha' he paid me, but sure I'm
not goin' to be tellin' them anythin'. They
can do nothin' 'cos I'm the age and so is the
punter and the two of us knows what we are
doin' and there's nothin' they can do unless they
see the money changin' hands.' (Brian, rent boy)

Thus, in the Phoenix Park and other areas where street
prostitution is common, the gardaí may find it difficult to
secure a conviction. The client and prostitute may also
claim that they are two consenting adults and that there
is no money involved:

> You see, when we get two fellas driving up in
> the car, chances are that they are just boy-
> friends because the gay community tend to
> go into the Park as well. The only way we
> can be sure is if we know the fella to be a
> rent boy, but again this can be difficult to
> prove in court. (Garda 1)

> We can police an area where we know the
> prostitutes hang out. We can watch them
> make a pick-up, we can even follow them,
> but if they go into a private apartment or
> house, we have no reason to question them.
> We cannot enter the house without a warrant,
> and once one is obtained, presumably the
> transaction will be completed. (Garda 2)

An extreme lack of resources also contributes to the problem of controlling male prostitution:

> We would need so many men in order to properly police the whole of the Phoenix Park, we would need much more manpower. The resources and the manpower are just not there. (Garda 1)

Both street and off-street prostitutes are often prepared to oblige sadomasochists, but in Irish law, as in English law, a person cannot give consent to sexually stimulated physical assault. A case was successfully brought in England in 1990 against fifteen men who were involved in unpaid, consensual S&M. The men received severe prison sentences. According to The *Times* newspaper, the judge stated that 'the courts must draw the line between what is acceptable in a civilised society and what is not.'

On 21 February 1996, the Minister for Justice, when questioned in Dáil Éireann regarding the number of men and women prosecuted for prostitution under the Criminal Law (Sexual Offences) Act of 1993, stated that 12 men and 116 women had been prosecuted for various offences under the Act between 7 July 1993 and 31 December 1994. No later statistics have been made available.

At present, the gardaí appear to manage rather than prosecute male prostitution. An attitude of tolerance has been born among many gardaí. According to Raymond Byrne:

> There is always a discretion given whether the law will be enforced or not and how it will be enforced at different times. It's very

open, in a sense. The laws didn't change really but the attitude of enforcement and of the gardaí did.

Many of the gardaí are developing better relationships with the men involved in street prostitution; this is reinforced by the number of times they come into contact with them. So, the more experienced gardaí appear to be more tolerant of male street prostitution:

> When I first came to the Phoenix Park, I was amazed that male-to-male prostitution existed. I'm from down the country and I'd mention this kind of stuff at home and they'd be in shock, but now I see it every day and you just get more used to it and you begin to understand it. I have no real interest in arresting them. My mentality would be, I wouldn't mind arresting the clients but not the prostitutes. I would prefer to go, 'How are you and what's your name', and take their names. You see, the names go into a book and the majority of names of clients that you take into the book will not appear again. You would get the rent boys in the book over and over again but not the clients. The client who is caught and gets his name in the book, he is shitting for weeks afterwards. He doesn't know why his name has been taken and why it is in the book and that is usually enough, especially for those fellas going up there in their BMWs, they don't want any trouble with the law. They might be moving on

somewhere else but they won't get caught in the same place again. Many of them have wives and families to think about and some have considerable social status. (Garda 1)

Further confidence needs to be built between the gardaí and the male prostitutes so that the prostitutes might be encouraged to report assaults by clients:

I wouldn't report it [an attack by a client] in a fit 'cos I'm not supposed to be working as a rent boy so if I got a batterin' I wouldn't go to the Old Bill [gardaí] 'cos they'd be havin' no sympathy for me and all. (Brian, rent boy)

The gardaí need special training in the area of prostitution and need to be educated about the exit strategies available to those who are involved. There is little coordination between garda stations, little, if any, exchange of information, and inadequate allocation of resources:

There isn't enough push from high up in this job to combat the problem of male prostitution. There was a vice squad in the Phoenix Park years ago and they took it off. The vice squad did arrest people up there because they had to; they were given orders. I think this should be set up again. If this happens there would be arrests because it's like a drug squad. You must produce a return of work. This would be needed all over in order to combat the problem. Having said that, however, this problem won't be solved by the gardaí working in isolation. We need help from the other organisations that come into contact with male prostitutes . . . It needs to be a group effort. (Garda 1)

Paul Flynn of Crosscare, which provides an emergency and aftercare service for homeless boys, added:

Not a lot of resources are pumped into this by the gardaí. It is not a big issue for them. Prostitution is not a big issue. They don't have a vice squad and we have one sexual assault unit for the whole country, which is an absolute disgrace, and that deals with everything from child molestation to rape, and how many cases are they getting in a day? It's a joke.

The criminalisation of male prostitutes exposes them to further dangers, making them more vulnerable. It may also lead to victimisation and prejudice. A more positive approach is needed which might involve referral to another agency for counselling or perhaps drug treatment. The emotional and social needs of the prostitute have to be addressed before any real progress can be made:

There seems to be a sad lack of cooperation between the health boards, social workers, gardaí and hospitals and those who are involved in cases such as male prostitution or criminal matters pertaining to the family, abuse etc. (Garda 2)

The legislation covering prostitution in Ireland is tangled and ineffective and an imaginative revision of it is required, which would establish separate provisions for children and young boys. Paul Flynn says:

> We have been trying to change the legislation. I mean the legislation still says that children have to make a statement, which is not going to happen. It will not happen because 99 per cent of them are criminalised anyway. They are involved in criminal behaviour because of their involvement in male prostitution. There are a lot of drugs involved in it and they don't have a relationship with the gardaí anyway, only a negative one. The child should be removed and a professional should be able to act on behalf of the child.

The criminal-justice system is not sufficient to deal with male prostitutes working on the street, in escort agencies and as self-employed masseurs. A structured referral programme prior to release from the garda station might highlight possible alternatives to a life of prostitution. Key professional groups and agencies working in the area of male prostitution need to be identified and encouraged to work in conjunction with the gardaí.

8

'MY DOUBLE LIFE'

THOMAS'S STORY

Thomas's family moved to Dublin from the west of Ireland when he was ten years of age. He is an only child. The move was very difficult for Thomas and he found it impossible to settle in his new school. He felt very alone at first, missing his old friends and country life. He began to rebel both at school and at home. He became involved with an older group of boys who accepted him because of his delinquency. He was seduced by a much older boy when he was thirteen and was rewarded with £5 for his acquiescence and his vow of silence. The sexual encounter was repeated. He was set up at an early age in a life pattern which was to persist into adulthood. Thomas feels that he has always been gay and enjoyed those early sexual engagements. At the age of eighteen, after leaving school, Thomas became involved in the hustling scene as an escort. He is twenty-three now and still living at home with his parents but does not have a very close relationship with them. They know nothing of his involvement in prostitution and he does not generally inform them of his whereabouts.

He is attractive, with long, fair hair to his shoulders. He has big, brown eyes and a wide smile. He is well-built and is under the impression that he is very well-endowed. He comes across as very confident and self-assured. He is quite selfish and unconcerned about others, especially his clients.

Thomas is always well-dressed. He talks constantly and does not give others a chance to speak. He is extremely pushy and opinionated and gets worked up in an argument. He loves to socialise and is very promiscuous but claims he is always careful. He does not plan to continue in prostitution all his life but hopes to be rich and famous, although he has no qualifications and no plans to further his education.

'They think I'm working as a sales rep for an insurance company; well that's what I've told them, anyway. I tell them that I work my own hours and that's why I have a pager, in case they need something done immediately. They probably don't believe me 'cos I do get paged at all hours of the day. I don't talk to them much and they've always let me do me own thing. I gave them an awful time when I was younger. I was always in trouble, getting suspended from school, annoying the neighbours. I was hanging around with this group of lads and we used to be up to no good the whole time. I was always mitching school, telling the teachers to fuck off and all that kind of stuff. I think the parents are just glad that I'm working and out of trouble. They don't ask me questions and I don't give any answers. I'm getting my own place as soon as I can, anyway, as soon as I get enough money saved. I've never told them I'm gay but they might suspect. If they don't, they're stupider than I thought. I've never had any girls around ever and always get calls from guys. One way or the other, I don't really care and I don't think they do either. If they were to ask, I wouldn't tell them, anyway.

'I used to hang around with this group of lads after school. They went to a different school so we'd often go mitching together. They lived in the next estate, most of them. They were into all sorts, trying drugs and smoking, and I would have been only eleven or twelve . . . They were older than me. There was one of them and he let me hang around with them 'cos I would always go first to do whatever we were getting up to. He fancied me anyway, he did. There was one day we were in one of the lads' houses during the day and there was no one at home and I think I would've been maybe thirteen and we were all looking at each other's dicks and playing with each other and this guy who fancied me took me into the other room and he started getting me to suck him off and he did the same for me. I had sex with him the first time. I remember he gave me a fiver and told me to keep my trap shut. He was gay but I don't think any of the other lads were because they wouldn't go off with him. We used to meet all the time for a quick shag. I was mad about him . . . It was him who showed me the ads in *Hot Press* about the escorts and he kept telling me I'd be good and that I could make a lot of money. I think he went for them as well but they didn't take him 'cos he wasn't as good-looking . . .

'I phoned the number and the interview was set up . . . I was asked all sorts of questions in the interview. I knew the score, though, before I went because I had been told. I was asked me height, me age, what I'd do, was I gay or straight and then they had a look at you starkers [naked]. I think he was surprised when he saw my dick. They took me on because I have a huge dick. I mean it's really big. Many of the fellas that come in here pick me and once they have me they'll always come back for more. The agency values me. I'm the best guy they have. They also want you to be clean and all. They don't take smelly bastards in.

'The agency arranges the date, the time and the location with the client over the phone. They ask them what kind of guy they want, what age, what colour hair and what they want done. If they say they want a guy with a big dick, I'm in there hands down. Then the person who takes the call will page me; all the escorts have the pagers so they can get them at any time. Most of the dates are for the evening time but there's some during the day and late at night as well. You could be just getting into bed and then they'll page you and you can't really refuse. The agency hates that. It can be a balls to your social life. You might be out in a club and next thing the pager goes off, so you have to be careful not to be drunk and all 'cos the client will complain if you arrive lamped out of your head [drunk].

'You do get your nights off as well, usually one or two in one week. When you meet the client, in my case, it's usually in their house or in a hotel 'cos I don't have me own place. When I do I'll be able to take those ones who can't bring the escorts home and can't afford a hotel. Imagine them landing into me parents' gaff, now that'd be some laugh . . . This is usually followed by a short chat; the shorter the better I always say, but I'm good at the shit talk to get them to relax. Some of them are well on edge and don't know what to be doing with themselves. I have to laugh at them. Some of the old geezers just love talking; they like the sounds of their own voices and they go on and on and on and you're just sitting there, nodding, wondering are they ever going to shut the fuck up. After that, I do ask the client what he wants done. Some of them want massage. I'm crap at them, but I do them if they ask. They do say what they want and I name the price. You have to make it clear that if he wants more than he has said, he'll have to pay for it. There's nothing for free when you're with me. Then he hands over the money. I usually go as far as him and maybe kiss him or feel him up. Then I'd open up my trousers and take out the 'big man' and then we'd both undress. Some of them would only want a wank or a blow. Everything they get done costs money, like a wank and a blow job would be about £30, for me to wank and blow him, but for him to do the same for me, that's more – about £50. Then if he wants the ride and all, that's £150 for me to ride him. For him to ride me as well, that would be £200. If I make £200, then £70 goes to the agency, a little over a third, and then the rest is mine. If you get a taxi home or anything, that comes out of your own money as well. Any weird stuff, like S&M, we don't normally do, unless of course the price is right. I have no problem whipping some fella if he wants to pay me for it . . . This fella gave me £100 once just to piss on him. He lay down in the bath and got me to piss on his face and body. It was filthy but as I said the money was right and everything has its price . . . Some of the clients are filthy rich – some of them would be well-known as well, like you might be seeing some of them on telly and everything, that's all I'll say. Most of them are married men, but you get the older fella too who can't get the ride without paying for it.

'Some weeks are better than others but I do all right. Some of the guys want to meet in the escort's home and

I obviously lose out there but I make enough money to keep me going. I have nice clothes and I can go out any time I'm off and I can go clubbing and get drunk, get a few E tabs [ecstasy], no problem. Anything I want I have . . . I'll soon have enough for me own place.

'I think I can go on doing it till I'm at least thirty, then maybe I might get some sort of a job. Who knows, maybe I will get a job in sales, like the job my parents think I have, or I might even set up my own agency and get rich. I'd love to open a gay club in the city but you'd need a lot of money to do that. I know one thing: I am going to be rich.'

9

'Reaching Out'

The Health Risks
and Services Provided

Male prostitution is a high-risk activity. Such risks are of
a physical or emotional nature and include assault, murder,
rape, robbery, drug abuse and every form of sexually
transmitted disease, including HIV/AIDS. In Ireland,
there is a myriad services that come into indirect contact
with men involved in prostitution. Such services include
organisations for the homeless and for homosexual men,
services for sexually transmitted diseases, including HIV
and AIDS, drug clinics, outreach services and aftercare
units. There is, however, a huge deficiency in the number
of direct support services and outreach workers and in
the degree of inter-agency collaboration. Whether or not a
fully specialised service for male prostitutes is required is a
matter of opinion, and people remain divided on the issue.

Outreach and detached work, i.e. drop-in centres, as well
as information and advice from voluntary workers, are
necessary to deliver educational messages and to enlist the
participation of male prostitutes in health checks and AIDS-
prevention strategies. Cooperation between the different

service providers and crisis prevention should be the essential elements of any male-prostitution service. Service providers are in a prime position to intervene in health promotion and coping strategies and cannot operate in isolation if they are to meet the complex needs of those working in the male sex industry.

In 1992, the Eastern Health Board was instrumental in setting up the Gay Men's Health Project (GMHP). It is partly concerned with men working in prostitution and offers a wide range of health-care services:

> The service is for gay or bisexual men, men who have sex with other men, and offers a drop-in clinical service twice a week. There is an HIV test, hepatitis B and C testing, counselling and free condoms. STD screening for gonorrhoea or whatever, that is also a big part of the service. I do outreach work and I work in the pubs and clubs giving out free condoms and information and I do some workshops. There is no specific service for men in prostitution and many of the young men we would have met would have been marginalised and would have found it very difficult to come to a service such as ours, so what we are doing at the moment is recruiting more staff, and hopefully I will have two more outreach workers and part of their brief will be making contact with those who are marginalised, including those involved in male prostitution. (Mick Quinlan, GHMP)

In terms of developing services, in my opinion, the provision of a specialised service for men in prostitution may serve to further disenfranchise those involved, emphasising the differences between these people and others for whom services are already available. Young people who are homeless or impoverished, who misuse drugs or whose health is at risk through ignorance and lack of awareness will have a lot in common with those engaged in prostitution. To separate the activities of the different agencies may only isolate those who work in the sex industry and contribute to the problem and the stigma associated with it:

> It is a case of how to provide the service. It's a bit like the STD clinic up in the Mater Hospital. Let's say it's every Wednesday, there is a prefab beside casualty, every person going in there is going for a test and everyone knows that everyone going in there is going for whatever and that in itself provides a barrier. I'm not sure if having a specific service is the way to go. In New York, the outreach service would be part of an overall outreach – it is not specific to prostitution . . . It's a bit like tackling the crime or tackling the causes of the crime. The causes of the crime today are essentially the need for money, primarily for drugs or alcohol addiction, so as long as the need for money for that is there, it will continue, so I suppose you need to remove the original cause before you can wipe out the male prostitution and that will involve tackling addiction problems as well.
>
> (Fr Feargal McDonagh, chaplain,
> Arbour Hill Prison)

While it has been argued that targeted health services for male prostitutes would enable health-risk behaviours to be monitored, it would be very difficult to get those at risk to attend because of the degree of negativity attached to their profession. Jesuit priest Fr Peter McVerry set up his first hostel in Dublin over twenty years ago. He has been working with homeless boys since then and now runs three hostels. According to McVerry:

> There are no services directly geared for young people involved in prostitution. Maybe that's as well because you don't want to label people. I mean, if you had a building that was for counselling children involved in male prostitution, no one would go there. It is probably better to have generic services, but it is virtually impossible to get a counsellor for someone who is abused or who has been involved in prostitution.
>
> The boys would come to us for help because they need somewhere to live, they may not necessarily be in prostitution. It's not just overnight – these boys may stay with us for two to three years so it becomes their home basically.

A number of male prostitutes engage in unsafe sexual practices and some are prepared even to indulge in unprotected sex if the punter is willing to pay more money. Knowledge of wider health risks among young male prostitutes, especially among those operating at street level, appears to be limited and fragmented:

If he [the punter] does be wantin' me to be
doin' the business with a johnny, it depends
on wha' he offers. If he is offerin' a lot of
money, then I'd probably take it.

(Brian, rent boy)

Many street hustlers have inadequate knowledge of health-
care issues and many are unaware of available services:

If I knew where to go to get the free johnnys
I probably would and all, you know.

(Mark, rent boy)

When prostitution is combined with other forms of
activity, such as intravenous drug use, or is accompanied
by homelessness and living on the streets, the health risks
for the people involved rise substantially. The reduction
of attendant risks to young people involved in prostitution
should be a key element in planning a response service. A
range of services that tackle the different factors that
precipitate involvement in male prostitution need to be
established:

We need to get services like ours to branch
out. We have to look at services for the
homeless and for drugs, needle-exchange
services, etc. I think we need to create
awareness of our service and of other services.
We need more agencies. We operate under
the Health Board and we have certain respon-
sibilities, and with other agencies we need to
decide what is the best way of providing
support for these people if they wish to give

up prostitution. A lot of it has to do with resources. (Mick Quinlan)

One of the greatest problems in getting male prostitutes to avail of services is the denial factor – the fact that they are unwilling to admit involvement in prostitution. While some of those involved in street prostitution are upfront and positive about their sexuality, others refuse to identify themselves to the services available for fear of legal and social recrimination. As a consequence, it can be very difficult to work with those who refuse to admit that they are 'on the game'. These men are potentially at greater risk than those who admit their involvement in prostitution, and it is much harder for workers to gain trust to engage with them and discuss issues relating to safety, safer sex and sexual health:

> There wouldn't be a huge number of them who would speak about it. The only ones who will talk about it are a little bit more mature and have a deeper insight into themselves and are able to see it in context. It's because the class they come from is so rigid in its stereotyping – male and female stereotyping – so it's a major thing for them to speak about it.
> (Fr Feargal McDonagh)

Harm reduction is not just about giving out condoms. It also involves working with young people on issues like building self-esteem and confidence so that they might be able to negotiate 'safe sex' with a punter when the time arises. It is almost impossible to reach those working in off-street prostitution such as self-employed masseurs and agency workers. However, since these people tend to be better educated, it is more likely that they will know about the dangers to their health. Those employed by agencies and massage parlours should be warned by their employers to observe safe-sex practices at all times and should be provided with free condoms. Confidentiality is vital to the process of developing a relationship with those involved in the hustling scene. It is also necessary for the service providers to understand the reasons why people get involved in street prostitution:

> When you get to issues like prostitution, there are a whole range of co-factors involved. There may be other issues, such as self-esteem and self-destructive behaviour, but I would need to learn more about those involved in order to fully understand.
>
> (Niamh Moynihan, Cairde)

Cairde was set up in 1985 to provide a support service for those who are HIV-positive. Crosscare is another service that has come into contact with young male prostitutes. It was set up in 1986 to provide emergency short-term care for boys. In May 1993, an aftercare support unit was set up to provide supportive and educational programmes to enable these young people to remain at home and to prevent their re-entry into homelessness. The aftercare unit aims to fight the evils of male prostitution and paedophile activity:

> Fifteen per cent of the boys that come to our service would have been involved in prostitution, so say one hundred boys go through

our service in one year, fifteen of them would have been involved in some way. It is a major problem, particularly in the past number of years, because it has gone underground. There needs to be more ground-root projects. When they get to residential care, the system has failed them. If they get to that point. I think we need to stop putting money into resident-ial care and start putting money into the pre-school services and into the local community – preventative work – and that's where the work really needs to be done.

(Paul Flynn, Crosscare)

Those at risk of involvement in male prostitution need to be reached before they can become established in the sex industry. Service providers need to operate from the perspective of understanding rather than moral condemn-ation. There is a lack of guidance for statutory social workers in this field and this must be addressed before the situation in Dublin can be remedied. There is also a dearth of resources available to the multidisciplinary approaches that have been set up:

I know of one case where a boy was waiting one year to receive counselling, and that's just ridiculous. We ended up paying privately because you would end up waiting forever otherwise and this problem needs to be addressed as soon as possible.

(Fr Peter McVerry)

Paul Flynn of Crosscare was equally critical of the lack of necessary resources:

> We are a very under-funded service. Aftercare is not seen as a strong part of the system. It is seen as something which is stuck on to the end of a service, in a sense.

Various practices associated with male-to-male sexual activity carry with them the potential for medical difficulties, including the danger of foreign objects introduced to the rectum (i.e. dildos and vibrators) and forms of sadomasochism. The anus, unlike the vagina, has no natural lubricating function and insertion of unlubricated objects can result in tissue laceration (Agnew, 1986). It is also quite easy to lose control of an object that is inserted into the rectum, particularly if it has been lubricated. Medical intervention may be required to retrieve the object and this can cause serious damage to the wall of the colon. Fist-fornication, which has become very popular among male prostitutes, involves the insertion of the hand, usually as far as the wrist and sometimes further, into the anus. This is another high-risk activity and is frequently engaged in by male and female homosexuals. It can cause severe damage to the anal or rectal walls.

In addition, sexually transmitted diseases are not restricted to the genitals and may be transmitted via anal activity. Examples include gonorrhoea, syphilis, anogenital herpes, hepatitis (A and B) and AIDS. Many street prostitutes have inaccurate knowledge about STDs and how they can be contracted:

> No, there's no need to be wearin' a johnny.
> You can't catch nothin' from suckin' a bloke
> off. (Brian)

Brian obviously does not realise that he can transmit or catch an infection through the throat. Fr Peter McVerry, however, believes that knowledge among prostitutes about health risks is improving:

> A lot of boys I would have dealt with a few
> years back would not have known about the
> health risks but today I would say they are
> much more aware than they used to be.

Since some of the male street prostitutes perceive themselves to be heterosexual but engage in homosexual activity, their lifestyles may place them at a greater risk of contracting and spreading STDs. The use of drugs and alcohol during sexual transactions can also lower inhibitions and may render participants more reckless. Programmes need to be established to address the problems associated with the male sex industry as it relates to the knowledge, treatment and prevention of STDs. This could be done as part of a generic service, which would educate and support them in making their health-education efforts more efficacious. While insistence on safe-sex practices appears to be more prevalent among the off-street prostitutes than among street prostitutes, Thomas's comments were a cause for concern:

> Yeah, I practice safe sex. Them blowing me
> is harmless and if I blow them it's low risk,
> very low risk. If I fuck them I always wear a

condom, if they fuck me, they use a condom and I don't let them come inside me. With fisting I would use a lubricated glove and I always wash my hands afterwards.

The treatment of STDs has, until recently, been deplorable. STD services in Dublin have been run as part-time services without any full-time staff. STD clinics were hidden away in secluded corners of hospitals and were labelled 'special clinics'. As a result, the taboo surrounding these diseases was reinforced by the attitude of the hospitals.

There is a need for a greater number of services to deal with the pressing social problem of male prostitution. There is also a need to discover workable rehabilitation methods because of the degree of drug abuse that tends to go hand-in-hand with prostitution:

For someone who is on drugs and involved in male prostitution, the first thing for them to do is clean themselves up. It is not just to end the chemical addiction. If someone undergoes a drug-treatment programme and he is clean and then released into the very same environment that is partially responsible for his drug problem in the first place, he is in an impossible situation. The Danish prison authority in the seventies had the drug problem we are having now. They started a project and they got this old schooner, the SS *Fulton*, and they put them on the SS *Fulton*, about sixty fellas in their early twenties for about six months at sea. They

were re-sensitised. There was a whole bond-
ing process and they left as a strong core
group. If you send them back to their original
environment you are placing an impossible
burden on them. You can't treat people
individually but in groups and you can em-
power them and provide an alternative. Like
when the crowd left the SS *Fulton*, employment and accommodation were sorted out
and they already had their own support base
and community and they were already linked
up with non-drug-using support families. We
would need something like that here.

(Fr Feargal McDonagh)

Little has been done by social service agencies or public-
health authorities to study male prostitution, which is on
the increase. The matter has been largely ignored in a
practice of group silence. Effective intervention with the
male-prostitute population must include acceptance of the
individual despite his lifestyle, and education as to the
risks and alternatives available:

If you are talking about prostitution, the only
way to reach them is to outreach them – you
meet them on their terms. The best way to
reach any community is to go out to them, to
mingle with them and become a part of their
environment, and then you become educated.
You meet people where they are and let them
know that it's OK. If you are in prostitution,
then that's OK – you have got a friend here
if you need one and leave it at that.

(James O'Connor, OpenHeart House, a
peer support group for those with HIV/
AIDS)

According to Paul Flynn of Crosscare, there are many
males who cannot be rehabilitated from a life of prostitution:

> There are some fellas you will never work
> with and you have to accept that, and this
> doesn't happen enough in this country – that
> there are kids who will not link into any
> services. They should be given the message
> that if you want to live on the streets, fine,
> but here is the alternative.

Men involved in prostitution are a stigmatised, marginalised and criminalised group and are likely to be mistrustful
of any intervention, particularly if it is perceived as
moralising or coercive. No agency can or should operate
in a vacuum, and cross-boundary work is vital to ensure a
strategic and productive response to those who have
embraced prostitution as a way of life. A more complete
understanding and acceptance of male prostitution in
Dublin is crucial to the development of effective statutory
or voluntary programmes to provide services to male
prostitutes. This group may be difficult to reach because
they are part of a subculture which is often separated from
mainstream society. There is a lack of proficient coordination between health, education and social services,
charities and the gardaí in dealing with the growing
problem of the male sex industry. Multidisciplinary
approaches offer the greatest potential for proper service

provision, since the needs of male prostitutes are many and varied. This should involve careful planning, coordination and commitment to resources. To date, the system has not been adequate in meeting the needs of those engaged in selling sex and now the time has come to redress those shortcomings.

10

'THE NAME OF THE GAME'

JOE'S STORY

Joe is twenty-five years old and has a university education. He attended University College Dublin (UCD) for four years. He previously worked as a masseur but decided for a number of reasons that meeting clients in gay saunas was a more viable option – lower overheads and more-flexible working hours. He has a full-time job in marketing and arranges to meet his clients in the saunas after 5 pm. Joe is gay and appears to enjoy what he is doing and loves meeting new people. He is intelligent, articulate, attractive and well-dressed. On most occasions when I met Joe, he was wearing a suit and carrying a briefcase. He does not want his colleagues at work to know about his prostitution and does not have any close friends among them.

While he is still in contact with his family, they have not been very accepting of his homosexuality. He has three sisters but does not get on very well with any of them. He wishes more than anything that his parents would accept that he is gay. He wants them to accept him for who and what he is.

Joe lives in a modest flat in the city centre and hopes

to continue what he is doing for as long as possible. He is a likeable character who seems to get on well with his clients and has a number of close friends in the gay community.

'When I was eighteen, I decided to tell my parents that I was gay. My dad couldn't handle it at all. It went against everything he believed a man should be. He's also into religion. I am his only son and he can't handle the fact that I am gay. He's not a violent man, but I will probably never forget the look of disgust on his face, the disappointment and the anger. I think he was angry at God more so than with me, for giving him a gay son. I think if I had told him anything else, he would have taken it better than he did. Mum was crying the whole time; that's what I remember about her reaction. I have three sisters as well. I think my older sister knew because she wasn't a bit surprised when I told her. The middle one didn't care at the time, because she was probably going through some crisis with one of her many boyfriends, and then the baby of the house was the best. Coming from a religious family like ours, with old-fashioned parents, I'm surprised by how liberal she is. I think she's probably fascinated by the thought of two men together.

'I don't think Dad has looked me straight in the eye since that day. He didn't reject me or anything – he just couldn't stand the sight of me after that. If we were sitting in a room on our own, he'd get up and walk out. It was like as if he thought I was going to come on to him or something. We always had plenty of money. My parents live on the south side of Dublin. I think that was another thing that killed Dad: he couldn't handle the neighbours

132

knowing, and all his golfing friends, that his son, the one he has been bragging about all these years, was gay. It was such a let-down for him. I suppose he had always imagined the speech he would make at his son's wedding, the one where he would stand up with that look of pride on his face and compliment my bride on how well she looks and tell me that I've always done the family proud. I suppose I can sort of understand where he's coming from. So when I started college in UCD, Mum suggested that I move out. "It'll be easier to get to college," she said, but I know it was because Dad wanted me out of the house and out of his life to a certain extent. Don't get me wrong – they've always supported me, paid for my apartment and my college fees. I was lucky that way but in all honesty, all I wanted from them was acceptance. That would have made me much happier.

'Even when I go and visit them now rarely, I might add – the conversation is kept to the weather and my job and a number of 'safe' things along those lines. We don't have any real conversations and they both seem constantly on edge when I am there. Dad is afraid the conversation might turn to homosexuality. There's days I'd love to turn around to him and scream, "Yes, I am gay, and guess what, I'm a prostitute as well." The only thing that stops me is that he'd probably die of shock. So I moved into the one-bedroom apartment which I had while I was in college. It was near UCD so it was very handy. One day I was just sitting there with this other gay friend of mine and he said, "This place is way too big for one person", and I got to thinking. I had seen numerous ads in *GCN* [*Gay Community News*] and in *Hot Press* and I knew the full extent of what was on offer, so it seemed like a good idea. I didn't know the first thing about massage therapy but I said I'd give it my best shot. I bought a step-by-step guide to the good massage and the necessary oils and that was it, really. I guess I learned it as I went along. I turned my room into a den of iniquity, so to speak, and I bought an old couch bed for the living room and I used that as my room. It was a cool idea really 'cos I knew Dad was never going to come over and when Mum would visit on those rare occasions, she'd always phone first and I'd make sure the place was presentable when she arrived. The couch bed was always folded up during the day so that was never suspect. We'd talk of college and how my studies were going and then she'd be on her way again. It was funny because any time she came she brought a pot of jam, of all things. I had a press full of jam and I hadn't the heart to tell her to stop bringing me jam. I think it was like her way of making a peace offering or something and every time she'd come she'd tell me Dad was caught up with work and was sorry he couldn't make it. I knew he wasn't coming and I knew why. I think he felt that by coming to my place it would all become a reality and as long as he didn't have to see me too often, he could go on pretending that everything was normal.

'I finished working as a masseur about two years ago now and to be honest I'm glad. I let the apartment go because I couldn't afford it any longer. I wasn't really making enough and I was afraid I'd be done by the guards. Some months would be great and you'd get loads of customers, then the next month would be real slow. You'd have no problem making the rent one week and you'd be screwed the following week. I have this place now and it does me nicely. I work from nine to five like everyone else, in a marketing job, and I go to the saunas to meet my clients in the evenings. I often go there straight from work in a suit and all. No one knows at work of this side of my life and quite frankly I don't want them to. Most of them know that I'm gay and that's probably enough for them to contend with for now. Most of my gay friends know; some approve, some don't, but either way, I don't care. I don't have time right now for a boyfriend. The odd time, I would go to The George or somewhere at weekends and meet up with someone but there's no one serious at the moment. I did have a boyfriend a while back and he knew what I was doing. He used to love getting a massage. He knew what I was doing and he had no problem with it.

'Obviously in the saunas I don't need to be paying rent. I can arrange to meet clients there and I have an ad in the classifieds saying that I want to meet older men for massage and fun and games and then when they phone, I arrange to meet them in the saunas. It's dead handy, really, and some of my clients prefer it that way as well, especially those that don't like going to people's homes: that can be a risk for the client as well as the masseur.

'I had a group of regulars from the time I was doing massage and when they phoned me I told them of the change of plan. I did lose some customers at the time – those who wouldn't be seen dead in the saunas: usually the ones who don't want to be seeing other gay men around them; they don't like seeing such open displays of intimacy, the ones who are not openly gay. These guys can't accept the fact that they are gay. They might even be married and all and have gone through their whole lives rejecting gay people, even though they know that deep down they are really gay. To cover it up and to reinforce their manhood, they reject all gay men. They'd be the kind who would be referring to us as dirty faggots and so on.

135

Then the feeling gets too much for them – it just takes over and they have to be with a guy. The feeling is that overwhelming. They just have to do it or otherwise they will go crazy and that's when they phone the likes of me. Some of the men are gay, but most of them are the older married types. There's a few lads in the saunas that I meet and they know if they are stuck, they can always pay me for sex. The management wouldn't be wanting the likes of me in the saunas, but because I usually meet clients there it doesn't affect anyone. If I was openly soliciting then that would probably cause ructions.

'Obviously you haven't been in one of the saunas. There's a fee for admission. That fee covers the use of all the facilities, such as the saunas and steam rooms. I go to them all. There's a lot of older guys with that married look about them in there. There's a café in there where you can have a cup of coffee and you pay £10-£20 for the use of the facilities on your way in. You go in the door and pay the fee and there's the café. It's actually a lot less seedy than people imagine. There's a television screen and settees and comfy chairs when you go in, then you can go upstairs and there's changing rooms, with lockers for your clothes, and there are showers and a sauna and steam room. It appears to be like any other sauna or steam room in a hotel or health club. Basically what happens is that the men go in there and they change. They take off their clothes and put on a towel, which is provided. They have showers . . . I hope. That is a major downfall, for me – Irishmen's hygiene, which is a major problem. They might just dip in and out of the shower and that doesn't get rid of the smell of BO. It's all over the cubicle when you go in. That makes me feel sick. I have some respect for myself and they obviously have none when they come in smelling like that. I mean, I'd be embarrassed if I thought I was smelling badly. There are loads of private cubicles, which basically consist of little rooms with a plastic bed where couples can go if they please. So what happens basically is that everyone walks around looking at each other and if they like each other, they'll go into one of the cubicles and have a shag. That's basically how it works .. In the steam room, you might be just sitting there with a client and there might be two fellas getting it on beside you. That is supposed to be done in the cubicles, not where everyone can see you. There'd be men masturbating each other and everything. It's not unusual to see that sort of thing and more . . .

'Some people become animals when they go in there. I mean there is this "dark room" as it is known, and who in the name of God would want to go in there, when you can't even see who is touching you. That's just downright disgusting. I think they basically become animals and then these men go home to their wives. I mean, I feel sorry for the women . . . Men go into the dark room and you can't see who is there because it's black and you've no idea who is in there or what they look like. If you go in there you are asking for it . . . Some of the other places have rooms where there's all this leather gear and you can strap a client to it, if he's into that, and whip him, that sort of thing. There are many of them out there who love this kind of stuff, more than you would think. I'm not really into that sort of thing but if my client requests it and is willing to pay for it, I might be convinced.

'I don't think there is any harm in what goes on in the gay saunas. It's all very innocent, really, and at least it's above board. It's a great place for a guy who wants to meet another bloke quickly and anonymously. I mean it's better than him going up to the Phoenix Park and picking up a young fella who is under age. It's a respectable place and a respectable business, where men can go to have a good time and men like me can go to make a few bob.'

11

'THE DILLY BOYS'

DONAL'S STORY

A lot of young males in Dublin make the journey to London when 'trade' becomes slack in Ireland. Male prostitutes are most commonly found in Piccadilly Circus and a surprisingly large number of Irish men can be found hustling among them. They go to London, where clients are in large supply and more money can be made. Some visit Piccadilly for a short period of time while others choose to stay there, enjoying the anonymity and the easy availability of drugs and men.

Donal is one Dublin man who made his way to London and became a male prostitute there. What is unique about Donal's story is not only that he worked in London but also that he plied his trade on the street back in the 1960s, a time when male prostitution took off both in Dublin and, to a greater extent, in London.

Donal was born in Dublin in the 1940s and is now forty-nine years of age. He was a chronic heroin addict but now lives in the west of Ireland, where he works as a barman. He's married with two children. He lived in London and worked as a rent boy for many years before coming home. He has also served a number of years behind bars. He moved to the west of Ireland under the Rural Resettlement Scheme in 1992 and has managed to stay off drugs for the past nine years. He is trying to put his past behind him and move on with his new life, but each day this proves to be a very difficult task.

I spoke to Donal a number of times over the phone before we met, and it was because of the intervention of a friend of his that he finally agreed to meet me. His greatest concern initially was that I would expose him and that his children would find out about his former life.

I first met Donal in his home. He told his wife the real reason I was there but told his children I was interviewing him about rural resettlement. He is a strong, well-built man who bears the hallmarks of a person who has had a rough life. He has a number of scars on his body and each one comes with a story. He welcomed me to his home and, while he was a little distrustful of me at first, he eventually opened the door to his past and gave me a glimpse of the kind of life he led. Every day is a struggle for Donal but he is a man who deserves admiration a man who was not afraid to walk away from his past into an unknown future. I wish him luck with his new life.

'I became involved in the scene when I was just sixteen. I ran away from home and went to London and I started working in Lloyds' coffee house, quite near Piccadilly. I met up with a couple of lads there who I knew from Dublin. It was around this time I started using drugs, mainly heroin. A lot of Dublin lads were using [heroin] at the time, so I thought, why not? There was this guy called Alan, also from home, who suggested to me one night that there was a great way of making money around Piccadilly, "a way of making easy money", he said. At that time, I needed money for my growing drug problem and I was well interested in finding out how it could be made. Drugs at that time were fairly cheap: you'd buy a gram of heroin for a pound. Mind you, that was thirty years ago now. So, anyway, I asked him how it was you could make the easy money and he said, "Why don't you go on the game like the rest of us?" Sure, I hadn't a clue what going on the game even meant.

'It's really horrible for me to have to talk about all this now, to bring it all back. It's something I haven't spoken about for a long time and something I try not to think about either. I find it very fucking hard to talk about all this shit.

'To make a long story short, I was shocked when he told me what it involved, but the truth is, I needed the money to buy drugs and I was willing to do almost anything. That's how bad it was for me then. It turned out, anyway, you could go off with a man or a guy and it was two pounds ten shillings, which would be £2.50 in today's money. You could go off with him for half an hour of whatever he wanted and it was £5 if you stayed all night. That's really how it all started for me.

'I can never really put my finger on the reason I ran away from home, but I remember asking my parents could I go to London to work for the summer because that's what some of my friends were doing, and they said no, so I just got it into my head that I was going anyway. I was sixteen at the time and as stupid as they come. It was 1960, just three or four months before my seventeenth birthday. Like, it's the type of thing I've been in counselling for numerous times over the past number of years and it has come up a lot but I never really dealt with it at all and I know now I'll never come to terms with it. You couldn't even imagine how difficult it is for me to talk about this again and revisit a part of my life I just want to forget. I really wish it never fucking happened. Sometimes, I look back and it's like a dream, like it all happened to someone else and it wasn't me, you know, and the fact that I'm heterosexual completely fucking does my head in when I think about it. Like, some of the guys who were on the game were gay and I'm not saying that makes it any easier . . .

'The first guy I went with, I was really fucking terrified. I was really petrified. Your man was a supervisor in some big warehouse in London and he brought me back there and it was really fucking terrible. I didn't know what he was going to do to me. He got me to masturbate him and then he was screwing around with me. After that night, it became kind of easy. There was another time, there was this guy and he was another businessman and he was really strong; this was one big guy and he actually said to me one night when we were on the train back to his place – we were in a small compartment – and he said, "You know I could kill you right now, I could murder you and no would know where you were or who you were." That really frightened the shite out of me when I thought about it afterwards because it was so true. I was lucky enough, I suppose. I didn't really encounter much violence – that was really the only time I was really scared. I was never attacked or anything and lots of the guys on the game in Piccadilly had very bad experiences.

'I did come across some really bizarre stuff in my time

142

– weird men with fucking weird ideas. There was some really weird stuff the punters wanted me to do. There was this one guy and he had the leg off a chair and he used to get me to stick it up his arse and this is what got the fucker going. There were a lot of these kinds of demands and I found, funnily enough, that most of them came from the wealthy clients – really, really wealthy people. There was this other guy who had an apartment in Park Lane and he was obviously a millionaire and he had this thing, he used to wear rubber waders and had this rubber sheet and he'd lie bollock-naked with his rubber waders on. Oh, Jesus, when I think back on some of the stuff I was asked to do, it makes me sick. These men got their kicks out of real weird shit . . .

'There were some really peculiar individuals out there as well, even at that time. Like there was this other guy called "Slave Tony" and he used to get guys back and he'd wash their feet and he used to masturbate while washing their feet – he was just really weird, into all that fetish stuff. I'm getting really freaked out just talking about this stuff. I think it's 'cos I haven't spoken about it for so long.

'I had regular customers at the time as well. Like, there was one guy who was some sort of baronet – Sir John something was his name – he was an absolute and total pervert. He was into bringing boys and their girlfriends or boyfriends back and having group sex with them all and he was known to pay a lot of money. He paid about £10 or £20, which back then was a fortune. Most of the clients were married men, which I thought was really bizarre at the time, but then it was down to my own fucking naivety because I was so naive, like I didn't know anything about anything. I hadn't a clue. I didn't even know that gay meant homosexual. I was completely green.

There was this regular I had and he lived in Knightsbridge and he had a couple of shops and he was married and I didn't cop on for ages. I found out by accident one morning when I went to his shop and I saw him bringing his kids to school and, like, I was fucking flabbergasted. There was quite a few married men that I knew. I think most of them were really gay deep down and thought they could get away from it by getting married. I'd say they thought if they avoided it, it would go away, but of course that's not how things work.

'The other thing I didn't have a clue about was safe sex or AIDS or using protection or anything like that. Again, that was my naivety. I didn't know what sexually transmitted diseases were and I can guarantee most of the guys didn't either. I absolutely never used any precautions whatsoever – nor did any of the lads I knew. But, having said that, I never allowed anyone to have anal sex with me, you know, I just wasn't into it, even though you could get more money if you did it. There was this one guy, a rich American called Henry, he was from Connecticut and was with a guy from Thailand who was a senior politician, he was some minister or something. We were introduced one night in Piccadilly and he brought us off to what was a really exclusive restaurant at the time – Hatchett's restaurant – and he was in London for two weeks and the guy from Thailand was nuts about my friend Tommy so they paired off, so to speak, for the fortnight, and I was with this guy Henry. He spent a colossal amount of money on me every day for the two weeks, buying clothes and drugs and everything. His thing was he liked to take photographs of young boys in swimming trunks. He wanted to have anal sex with me and I was actually very tempted to give in to him but for some reason, thank God, I didn't. That was the only time I came close to doing stuff like that. He was offering me a lot more money, as well, but I didn't and he ended up asking me had I any friends who would oblige. So, I actually ended up getting another Dublin guy, who is now dead, to do the business with your man. I remember he gave him £150, which was like getting £2,000 now. It was so much money, so I did think twice about it – that amount of money would have bought a lot of drugs . . .

'Some of the clients I remember were actually nice guys, believe it or not. Some of them were just lonely old men. There were of course one or two nasty ones about, but I was lucky enough to avoid them. The average client would be about forty. They would rarely be much younger than that. There was one young guy in his twenties who was from a really rough area at the time – King's Cross – he was a nasty piece of work. I went with him one night and I remember hearing afterwards that a couple of guys went with him and they beat the shit out of him because he was well known for bringing rent boys back and not paying them you know, or beating the shit out of them and riding them when they didn't want to, and all that. I was lucky enough not to come across bad situations like that.

'It didn't always work out for me that I got to take the heroin before going on the game. If I did, it was great. Nine times out of ten, I was sick, anyway, and I needed the money so I'd have to go on the game, which made it even worse. Like, I mean, I would have done anything to get my next fix, anything – like, I even got into the scene of robbing queers. It's called turning them over. Like, if I saw someone I thought was an easy target, I'd beat the shit out of him and take his money. I did some time in

England for 'rolling' a homosexual. I got sentenced to eleven months for that but most of my convictions in Ireland were for breaking and entering – stealing just to feed my drug habit.

'I remember my worst prison sentence – I can easily say this was the greatest nightmare of my life – it was in Dundrum. Course, I got conned into going there because I was sentenced to St Patrick's Institution in the first place. Anyway, I went to Dundrum and it was an awful place. There was a twenty-foot wall around the yard and there was very little place for exercising. I remember being out there one day and I just freaked out, because it was so confined. I climbed up on the roof in some sort of protest. I was only nineteen at the time and I spent the day up on the roof and that got into the papers. My name wasn't mentioned but everyone in town knew who it was. That really upset my parents. I spent six weeks there and I'll never forget a minute of it. It was hell on earth.

'When I was released from there I went back to London. This was around 1969 or 1970. I had finished with the meat-rack scene in Piccadilly and I was engaged in petty criminal activity, house breaking mostly. At that time, I was using a drug called methadrine, which was my drug of choice. It's pure speed and you get it in ampoule form and you crack the ampoule and pour it into tea and drink it or you can inject it It's pure speed. I remember staying awake for days on it and I had massive hallucinations – one very common hallucination is you think any little bit of dirt, let's say under your nail or whatever, on methadrine, you constantly imagine the dirt is a bug. It's called 'met bugs', and this is scary stuff. One day, I remember, I was off my head and I had myself convinced that there were a load of met bugs under my skin so I got a nail and dug a hole in my hand to try and get them out. I remember another time when I got crabs and I didn't know what they were, I convinced myself they were met bugs so I shaved myself, my head, my eyebrows, my legs, my pubic hair, the lot, and I got into the bath with a Brillo pad and I scrubbed myself. There was lumps of flesh hanging off me. That was a very common hallucination at the time. That will give you some idea of how fucked-up on drugs I was at the time and when I'd be coming down, I'd be so low, I'd do anything to get more drugs, just to get rid of the sick feeling, you know. That's how bad it was . . .

'After a couple of years in London, I came back to Ireland and I got into trouble here and I did a longer spell of eighteen months in prison. While I was in prison at that time, my girlfriend, who had a baby for me – this was April 1975 – she was on her way to see me in jail and she was killed in a car crash, so I used that as an excuse when I got out to continue getting out of my head. I was out of prison five weeks when I met my first wife, Mary. She was from the south-east and she was a nurse and the fact that she was a nurse, I thought this was brilliant – more drugs – and she used to rob stuff from the hospital to give to me and she actually set up one of the hospitals so that I could rob it. That marriage lasted four years. I got married in April 1977 and in 1979 I left. I just walked out and went to Jersey and I was there for a couple of years and then came back and met my present wife. Course, I came back to another prison sentence. It was when I got out of prison after that, that I met my present wife. She is the best thing that ever happened to me. After I met her I stopped getting into trouble and I stopped fucking around and tried to get my life in order

– well, to the best of my ability, anyway. She knows about the rent scene. And then there's my friend Paddy: he's the only other person – and then maybe one or two people I met in treatment – who knows of my past. I remember when I told my wife, I remember she was really shocked and I suppose like a lot of other people who are not au fait with the scene, she assumed I must be queer. But then her own sister died of AIDS – she was a drug user as well so at least she knew pretty much what lengths people can go to, so I guess she understood how I got involved in prostitution. She had seen her own sister do almost anything for drugs, so she knew about the kind of addiction involved. It's fucking horrible to look back at it and when I think of my own son who is now sixteen, I think, Jesus Christ, he may be a big lad for his age but he's only a child and that's all I was when I first got involved in the rent scene. Like, I was only sixteen years of age and as green as the grass.

'Tommy, the guy from Dublin who was on the game with me – there was a good few Dublin guys working in London, but this guy Tommy was an addict as well – and he said to me one day, "Do you realise when we go back to Dublin, we're fucked; the easy money will be gone", he says, "What are we going to do?" and I didn't really think about it much at the time but like, in hindsight, it was a very astute observation on his part, you know – that we were going to go back to Dublin and have no drugs or money. Of course, when I did come back home, I went on a spree of breaking into chemists and dispensaries, just looking for drugs of any kind to feed the habit. I just had to have them, the feeling was so bad when I was sick. I'd have done anything to feel normal again, or what I thought was normal, anyway. That lasted another couple of years.

148

'The scene was really big in Piccadilly at the time. It's hard to believe this was going on in the sixties, but it was. Any night, there'd be about forty guys on the game – all young fellas, "chickens", they used to call them. There'd be at least forty every night – at least. And each of them would pick up a client. There was a colossal trade. It was like Woolworth's, you know, you just went in and picked the one you wanted: "I'll have that one there, please." It was just like that – the clients walked around and picked out the ones they wanted. There were so many clients that we could actually pick out our clients as well, as opposed to the other way around.

'Just to give you a picture: in Piccadilly Circus, there's a huge railing and it's like an alcove or a balcony or even a shelter. The railing would be about sixty feet in length and the boys would just hang over it and the guys would obviously park their cars elsewhere and just walk around. The thing back then was – it was all so corny – a guy would come over and just ask you for a light and if you caught his finger as you lit his cigarette, it meant you were okay. It gave him the indication he needed that you were on the game. Nine times out of ten, we would head back to their apartment or house or whatever. Sometimes it might be a hotel. One time I remember being brought back to the army barracks – this guy was a sergeant in the army – then other times, we'd just do the business in the car.

'There was never any interference from the police. Never in all the time I was there was I ever hassled by cops. They never came near us. They all knew what was going on. The odd time you might get a new fella or a bobby walking along and everyone would kind of clear off or start smoking or acting real butch, you know.

'I never came across any massage parlours or escort

agencies at that time – I don't believe there was anything like that going on at the time, but then again, I was very naive. There was one place I heard of but never visited: it was a place that had Turkish baths. I think most of the lads that went there were queer. There was no real pimp scene either back in the sixties. It was every man for himself; you were freelance. Mind you, I did a bit of pimping myself of a couple of girls after I left the meat rack. I would have been maybe twenty or twenty-one at the time. It brought in a lot of money, which I needed for drugs.

'My days were pretty much the same: on an average day, I'd get up at around ten or eleven o'clock and go around to the Wimpy for breakfast. I don't know if that place still exists. Then I'd get a tube to Piccadilly and basically hang around for the day in Piccadilly Circus, around at the statue, and if we had the money we'd score some heroin. There was a place we used to go to and use the toilets and we'd inject there. There was also a twenty-four-hour café on Piccadilly and we'd go and sit in there and at around seven we'd be over on the meat rack and we'd be hanging around, hoping for business. Some nights you'd be really lucky: you might get a guy and get £10 in an hour and that would be it, you'd be finished for the night. Some of the guys also had sugar daddies who were exceptionally rich guys who looked after them. There was one guy who had an orange plantation in Spain. He was absolutely rotten with money – he had so much money, he used never carry change. If he was given change, he used to fuck it away. He bought a sports car for this guy Tommy, a friend of mine, and he brought another guy over to Spain on holidays. He just had so much money, it was unreal. He dished it out like cornflakes and he always had a huge wad of money and he carried it in his breast pocket. He'd have loads of £5 and £10 notes and he'd be handing them out all night. We used to love seeing him coming.

'And there was this other guy – this was an interesting one. He was an American policeman. I don't know who introduced him to Alan – that's the guy who first told me of the game – and anyway Alan came along and told me your man fancied me. He was staying in the Regional Hotel so he brought me and Alan around to this Indian craft shop and he bought us two whips and brought us back to his hotel room and got us to lash the back off him. And he wasn't satisfied with that: he got a towel, a wet towel, and put a knot at the end of it and got us to beat the shit out of him with the towel. This guy was so sick, he used to eat shit sandwiches. This is how bad he was – I remember one night he took about ten of us out for a meal and his party trick was we were all allowed to stub our cigarettes out on his face, and this was in a restaurant. There was no ashtray needed at our table! He was a sick bastard and then he was saying to Alan one night when he was trying to get him to hit him harder – Alan was just tipping him with the whip – and he said, "Can't you goddamn hit me harder, your mother is only a fucking cocksucker anyways", and then of course Alan hit him and then he'd say, "For fuck's sake, I'm paying you guys for this, back home the boys come around and do it for fucking nothing." He was a sergeant, if I remember correctly, in the New York Police Department and he was giving us about £10 a go just to beat the shit out of him. Anything kinky like that, you could charge extra. The ordinary client would be charged £2 and ten shillings and that was for masturbation or whatever and if you stayed overnight it was a fiver, you know, so we were doing quite well. My rent at the time was £7 a week, which was expensive at the time in Earl's Court. I thought this was really expensive, that was back in the sixties. Mind you, Earl's Court was a very sought-after place at the time. It was a real exclusive area. In a good week, I could have made up to £100. That was a huge amount of money at the time; that would be a couple of thousand now. A pint was about twelve pence then. In old money that was one and eight pence, so that will give you some idea of the kind of money we were making.

'I was on the game for about eighteen months in all in London and it was basically to feed my heroin habit, as I didn't really have any other way of making money – working in Lloyds' coffee shop wasn't going to keep me going and give me the money I needed to buy my drugs. I was only involved in London. I never got involved in Dublin, although it was going on there as well, but the lads used to go to London when things got slow at home. They said it was much easier to make money. I thought that to get involved in the Dublin scene was just too close to home. I just didn't want to get involved, or be seen to be involved, either. I suppose it was a kind of a real closet scene in Dublin; not many people knew about it. I used to drink in the gay bars in Dublin when I came back. At that stage, we weren't into selling ourselves. We just hung around for the craic, you know, to have a bit of a laugh. Course we were still on whatever drugs we could get our hands on. I did a lot of time in jail because of breaking into chemists. As it turned out, London wasn't far enough away, either. It got back to my parents what I was doing and that really upset them and me. My father just couldn't believe it. When I got home he took me straight to a psychiatrist because he thought I was a bit nuts, you know.

'When I left London, I moved back to Dublin, and I can tell you my parents weren't very impressed by all I been up to, particularly because I suppose at that time Dublin was a very small community and everyone knew everyone else back in the sixties and stuff was in the paper for all to see. We were living in the city centre. I was from a working-class family, but my parents were very respectable. I even got to go to secondary school, because I was the youngest. There's a ten-year difference between me and the next child in the family. My father worked all his life; he was never out of work. He didn't drink much. Like, it was a pretty good upbringing really that I had, but I couldn't say I was particularly happy either, though. I mean, my father was pretty strict and my mother was very strict and, no, I really didn't have a very happy childhood. For instance, I had my own bedroom growing up, but I was never allowed put posters on the walls or anything because it made the room look untidy – you know, that sort of shit. My mother was a freak like that, you know. She was a head case when I think back on it. She had a cleaning fetish – you had to take your shoes off when you came into the house and she wouldn't have carpet because she said it gathered dirt; she had linoleum, which she polished every day, down on her hands and knees, scrubbing. Now, I mean she scrubbed and she polished like a madwoman. She wouldn't have a washing machine because she thought it was the devil's invention. She used to have a washboard and a big aluminium tub to do all the washing. I don't really have any other memory of her but scrubbing and giving out. She was very strange in that way. I think she had a chip on her shoulder because her family was fairly wealthy and it was considered a step down when she married my father, you know, and she had a chip on her shoulder then for the rest of her life.

'I had no freedom whatsoever when I was growing up and I really think that's why I rebelled against it and decided to run away. They did come looking for me and all. They spent five weeks in London just walking around, trying to find me, hoping to find me, and then of course when I was locked up they came to visit me. That was the first time they saw me since I ran away, locked up behind bars. I'm sure I broke their hearts.

'When I came back from London, only a few people knew what I was up to. The only reason my parents knew is because a friend of mine at the time told them. You see, when I ran away from home I'd try to steal money from my sister – £80 – but my mother came in as I was taking it and I stuffed it into a cushion in the settee and I ran away that night and I left the money behind me and I was telling this guy I knew from Dublin about the £80, which was still in the cushion, and on a visit home to Dublin, he decided to go to my house to try and find the money, and my mother was there and he said he was a friend of mine so she let him in and he started telling her what I was at over in London, and he was trying to sound all concerned and everything. He told her all about me going on the game. He also told her I was a drug addict as well. I'd say she nearly died. But, apart from my parents, only a few people knew about what I got up to in London. I have one brother and he doesn't know anything – he's older than me – and my sisters know nothing either. Obviously, they knew I was a drug addict, but that's about it. My kids know nothing about the rent scene either. My own family and my wife's family know I spent a lot of time in jail, and for this reason I felt I had to tell my son a little bit about my past. He was only twelve when I decided to tell him about being a drug addict and being in jail. I remember we went for a walk and I told him about the heroin and he was very upset and he cried bitter tears for the day but he has come to me since a few times to talk about it and I'm so glad that he feels he can come and speak to me about it all. I suppose telling him opened his eyes a little. He seems to have a very mature attitude to drugs now. He's really sporty as well. My daughter doesn't know at all. I've never mentioned it to her – I don't think I could – but I'd rather she heard it from me or the wife than from someone else.

'After I got home, it took me a long time to get away from the drugs. I only stopped using drugs nine years ago. I was on heroin for the best part of twenty years. I went into the Rutland Centre in Templeogue for treatment. It didn't stop me using drugs but it made me take a deeper look at myself and my behaviour. My first marriage broke up in 1979 and then in 1982 I met my present wife. She's from Dublin as well, from the inner city. She's a very strong person and I think I can say that a lot of my recovery was down to her. I was on heroin when I met her and I continued on it and maybe I'd get about six months clean and then I'd start using again, and then I'd get another six months clean, and that continued over the years, and then in 1988 I came across a doctor who was prescribing naps – morphine sulphate tablets – and I used to get a prescription of one hundred tablets a week off him and I was using only about four a day and I sold the rest. I got £20 for each tablet I sold so I ended up making quite a lot of money out of it in 1988, 1989 and 1990. I was still in Dublin at this stage and then in 1992 I saw this thing in the paper about rural resettlement.

I was on my way into another treatment centre at the time called Aiséirí for a period of six weeks of intense counselling and therapy and I saw this thing in the paper, and I know now when I look back I was totally deluded in the reasons for wanting to move down the country. I was thinking, I'm going to get away from it all and start a whole new life and everything is going to be great, really rosy like. I didn't take anything into consideration, like working or how I was going to live, or anything, and I wrote off and got a letter back when I was in Aiséirí, so we went down to see the house and decided we would take it. At first, we were renting a very small house, just the one up from the one we are in now.

'When I moved down the country, I couldn't get access to drugs. That was one of the main reasons I made the move, and another reason was the kids. Now, when I look back, I like to think it was the kids, but at the time, I think it was all to do with selfish reasons, for myself, and I knew when I came down I'd find it very hard and I did slip once or twice since I came down. I went up to Dublin on the odd occasion and used a couple of times – I'd say about five times, at least, but that would be at least nine years ago. I'm now nine years clean at this stage, like I don't even smoke hash now.

'I remember missing the money most and the access to money when I came back to Dublin. I had a great lifestyle in London. I always had money and I was able to dress well and all that. I spent money on myself and that's why when I came home I had to turn to other ways of making money. I smuggled heroin into Ireland a few times and I never got caught. The first time, I think it was only two ounces, but I had them stuffed up my arse and then I brought back larger amounts after that. I once walked through customs with a briefcase with a half a kilo of heroin in it in the airport, coming from London to here. Well, it actually came from Amsterdam but I picked it up in London and brought it back here. I was just bringing it back for someone else. I also brought hash back from Amsterdam to sell a few times. These were just some of the ways I made money. I often marvel when I look back at all the stuff I did and I wonder how I am still alive. I mean, when I look back at my past, it's like it's someone else, and I think to myself, "Who was that person?" I think that couldn't have been me, particularly now. I'd shit myself totally if I was to go through customs with a bottle of illegal whiskey, never mind a kilo of hash or a half a kilo of heroin.

'Of the Dublin guys I used to hang out with in Piccadilly, one of them is now involved in the Merchants Quay Project, the drug centre in Dublin. There's another guy there as well and they are completely off the game and off the drugs. Like myself, it took them an awful long time, a desperate fucking time. It took years really, like. One of those guys had the same kind of tough life I had: I think his wife died. It was terrible how his life went from one fucking disaster to another. I don't think he went for treatment or anything. I think he just managed to stop. He probably did do a detox programme and got on methadone. I think he may have substituted drink for the drugs for a while, and as far as I know he has stopped drinking as well. I remember another guy – he was Alan's older brother – he came over to London to bring Alan home and he got caught up in drugs himself and he actually drowned in the Liffey about ten years ago. He was selling stuff on the bridge and £20 flew over and he went down the steps to try and get it and he fell in and drowned. Jesus, I could go on all day about the people I knew and people who died as a direct result of drug abuse. Not many of the Irish guys got out of the game when I did and some of them that went back home went on the game in Dublin. I'm sure some of them are still alive now and they're probably still using heroin – they obviously wouldn't still be selling themselves because they'd be about forty-nine or fifty now; that'd be really peculiar. There's another guy I knew who was homosexual – I haven't seen him in about fifteen years – he lived outside the city, and I think he was into rent boys himself. When he was about thirty, he used to go up to the Phoenix Park and pick up the young fellas and he used to go to the toilets on O'Connell Bridge, but I haven't seen him in ages. I have no idea what he's up to now.

'I really think something has to be done about the scene in Dublin. I think there should be more help out there for those involved, more services, particularly for those who are homeless, and there are so many homeless kids who are on the game and their lives are in jeopardy. Apart from the obvious things like AIDS, these kids could be attacked and harmed. As dangerous as it was when I was on the game, I'm sure it's even worse now.

'To legalise prostitution would be a big mistake, in my opinion. You have to have normal people who know what they are doing, but most people who are on the game do not. They come from dysfunctional families and have horror childhood stories. Most of them, that is, not all of them – my family by most definitions would have been normal, and look how I turned out.

'I'm at the stage of my life now where I'm deeply embarrassed and ashamed of my past and I wish I could just wipe it out and say that it hadn't happened, possibly because I'm living down here. I'm now living a pretty normal life. That's the reason why I'm constantly amazed when I look back at my life. I have very low self-esteem now, because when I look back I think of myself as fucking shit; that's what I think of myself and that's how I feel when I look back.

'I wouldn't be bitter towards the Dublin lads who introduced me to the rent scene, because Alan, the guy who introduced me to it, was another drug addict, and he was a good friend of mine before we ever went to London and we looked out for each other. I wouldn't blame him, because nobody forced me into it. When I look back now, I'm just sad, very sad, that it happened to me. I often wonder why I was singled out.

'I'd never look back and miss my former life. I just hate that part of my existence and I wish I could erase it. I wouldn't go as far as to say I'm happy now, but I am reasonably content. I enjoy my lot in life now. I'm lucky to be alive and I have a wife who is just brilliant and two lovely children. I have a kip of a house but it's mine. I have a job and I have achieved a certain amount of respectability and I'm learning how to fit back in, which wasn't easy. It was very hard to give up the drugs and the gay scene and it's very hard to fit back in, I can tell you that.

'I found it very difficult to get close to people after I left the rent scene. I don't trust people. I have one close friend but that's all. I would be friendly with people in a superficial way but I would never take them entirely into my confidence. I'm always wary of people. I mean, I was used and abused for so many years that it became second nature to me. I mean, if someone offers me a drink, even now, I wonder what the catch is, I wonder why people are friendly, I wonder why they want to talk to me and what they want from me. The counselling has helped a little with this. It has enabled me to take a look at myself and my life. I was very rowdy about ten years ago. When we would go out for a night, I would always end up in a fight. I was also very abusive towards my first wife. I used to beat the shit out of her. I had so much anger inside me that I was unable to deal with it. I suppose I was angry at myself as well for allowing myself to become involved in the rent scene and allowing all that stuff to happen. It's quite possible that I was taking this anger out on others, but deep down I think I was just really angry at myself.

'Prostitution is an addictive lifestyle. When people get into it, they get used to the money and they sort of close their minds to what they are actually doing, and it's a lifestyle you just get hooked on. I mean, I really found it difficult to adjust to not having a constant supply of money, not being able to put my hand in my pocket and feel a wad of notes – that's something I haven't really experienced since I left the rent scene.

'To someone who is on the game now and on drugs, I would say to them to get into some residential drug-treatment programme. This business of going one day a week is no good, particularly because most of the kids are in deep shit and many are homeless, and going once a week is useless. They need to get in somewhere and have it drilled into them for six weeks at least and get it shoved down their throats what they are doing to themselves. They need to be shown that there is an alternative to the life they have slipped into. I was considering going around giving talks in schools – just to open children's eyes to the kind of traps that are waiting out there for them – but obviously my anonymity would be gone and I have to think of my wife and kids now. Anyway, I don't think I could relive the experience every day of my former life.

'I imagine the scene in London is still booming, as I imagine it is in Dublin too. I was on my holidays recently in Piccadilly and it was awful; it was really scary, really fucking scary. It was like I was hurled back into the past again. I saw quite a few lads hanging around there and it really hadn't changed all that much. I mean the style of clothes has changed, but that's it, really. The routine is still the same and even looking at the lads, they seemed somehow more brash and more confident and much more aware than I was. They are probably a lot more aware of the health issues as well.

'I'm really looking forward to my fiftieth birthday. My friend Paddy and I have a bet going because when I met him first, he said I'd be dead in two or three years because of the drugs – this was in 1988 – and I made a bet with him that if I was alive by fifty, he owed me fifty quid. If not, my wife would give him fifty quid, so all going well he'll be giving me fifty quid next year. I'm looking more and more like I'm going to win that bet and I can tell you, I'm very proud that I've made it this far, given the kind of life I've led.'

12

'QUESTIONS LEFT UNANSWERED'

THE FUTURE
OF MALE PROSTITUTION

There is an extreme paucity of published material on the subject of male prostitution in Ireland, and national data is largely unavailable. Indeed, there are no definitive or comprehensive studies of the male sex industry in Ireland. Knowledge of this industry in this country is limited and fragmented at best, ignored and misunderstood at worst. This is partly due to the fact that the practice is outside the boundaries of acceptable behaviour. But male prostitution does exist in Dublin and needs to be explored in greater detail. The prevalence of the industry in Ireland should not be underestimated.

The apparent upsurge in the number of male prostitutes seems to be universal. The male hustler is very much in evidence in England, Germany, France, Italy, Spain, Holland, Scandinavia, Asia and, of course, the United States. In Amsterdam, male prostitution services are more organised than elsewhere and are officially tolerated. Dutch society appears to be more broadminded when it comes to male and female prostitution than countries such as Ireland. In Amsterdam, for example, red-light districts have been established and brothels are licensed and advertise openly. The Dutch authorities aim to control prostitution within certain areas of the city. If a problem occurs with a client in a male brothel, then the police can be called by the male prostitute, without fear of imprisonment and fines. In this way, business is not driven underground and the health issues can be monitored and safe sex promoted in a better environment. This also allows the police to keep an eye on the activities of the male prostitutes and ensures that prostitution is not accompanied by other forms of criminal activity. In Denmark, Holland, Spain and Germany, magazines and videos, containing either homosexual or heterosexual pornographic material, that would be considered obscene in Ireland are openly sold. Berlin is another major home for male prostitution. It is also commonplace in Poland, Russia and Czechoslovakia.

In Asia, male prostitutes are available at very low prices and they are usually much younger than those found in other countries. In Japan, there are many male brothels and the boys working there may range in age from twelve years (the legal age of consent in Japan) upwards.

Studies of male prostitution appear to be most common in the United States, including New York (McNamara, 1965), and Boston (Allen, 1980). Many of these reports, and those from Britain, Poland, Sweden and Denmark, for example, emphasise the tragic psychosocial background of male prostitutes, with their high frequency of dysfunctional families, poor educational history and lack of training. Few consider the full extent of male prostitution.

It is notable that the clients of the male prostitute have not been studied in any great detail, and such a study has never been attempted in Ireland. Who are these people?

Why do they seek the company of male prostitutes? Are they predominantly married men who are inherently homosexual? To understand the male sex industry, both sides of the equation (prostitute and client) have to be examined. An in-depth look at the role that the demand for male prostitution plays in the creation and maintenance of the subculture would be advantageous.

The families of the male prostitutes are also an invisible population: there is no real means for them to express their feelings and meet with other families who are in similar predicaments. There are no specific support groups for them in Ireland. In addition, little is known about the lives of those who have survived involvement in the male sex industry. What becomes of them when they leave prostitution? Can they get conventional jobs? Can they lead normal lives? How do they cope? These are just some of the questions which need to be answered. Research into the extent to which male prostitutes drift in and out of the profession over a period of ten years, for example, would also be very interesting.

There are many different types of male prostitute and the dangers of making generalisations about them need to be highlighted. Those involved in male prostitution are not always runaways, delinquents or misfits. There are those who come from stable environments, who are well-educated, well-spoken and apparently happy. All types of prostitute exist in Dublin, on the street and off-street. A holistic approach needs to be taken when studying male prostitution because those involved have a wide range of needs. A man's involvement in prostitution can be seen as the result of the combined effect of a number of factors, which I have highlighted throughout the course of this book. Male prostitution cannot be attributable to any one factor. There needs to be a concerted effort to improve the overall quality of the lives of the people involved and to help them to make use of the alternatives. Help, management and acceptance of reality are the only remedies. It often seems, however, that male prostitutes, in particular, are the underserved 'backwater' and will remain so until there is a more general understanding of the reasons for their behaviour.

Outreach and educational programmes need to be put in place to raise awareness of male prostitution in this country. Existing programmes need to work together in order to reach those involved who want and need assistance. It is vital that initiatives are set up to inform the prostitutes, or 'sex workers', of the health risks involved, advise them of safer-sex practices and of the possible alternatives to a life of prostitution. A non-threatening and anonymous form of contact needs to be established between those in prostitution and the service providers. Male prostitution is a complex social problem. Currently, it remains largely ignored, as homosexuality, child abuse and domestic violence were in the past. It is time to address male prostitution and realise that the need for immediate and practical work in this area is paramount.

The law is unlikely to succeed in putting an end to male prostitution, so other options need to be explored in keeping it under control. One of the many effects of the legal system in Ireland has been to drive male prostitution underground, so careful revision of the legislation would be beneficial. The more male prostitution is outlawed, the more it will be associated with criminal activity. Regulation of male prostitution, as takes place in some other countries, is possibly a better control mechanism than attempted oppression.

Men in prostitution in Ireland have been virtually invisible. There is an absence of national policy on male prostitution. Coordination between the various agencies has been almost nonexistent. The law criminalises the prostitutes and society stereotypes them and is prejudiced against them. They infuriate gardaí, confound psychiatrists and bewilder legislators. Ireland has been slow to take on useful ideas from Europe and therefore male sex workers remain excluded and silenced. It is clear that no single agency has the power, resources or ability to respond effectively to the diverse experiences and needs of men involved in prostitution. Statutory and non-statutory organisations need to work together in a coordinated way. There needs to be an organised response to both the prevention of male prostitution and effective intervention when men are already engaged in the trade. It is a moral, educational, legal and health issue.

I hope that those who are prepared to deal with complexity, ambiguity, fluidity and uncertainty will find this book of interest as an attempt to understand a fascinating, intricate and often tragic aspect of human experience.

SELECT BIBLIOGRAPHY

Aggleton, Peter, Davies, Peter & Hart, Graham (1990) *AIDS – Individual, Cultural & Policy Dimensions.* The Falmer Press.

Agnew, Jeremy (1986) 'Hazards Associated with Anal Erotic Activity', in *Archives of Sexual Behaviour*, 1986, vol. 15, no. 4, pp 307–314.

Bagley & McDonald (1984) 'Adult Mental Health: Sequels of Child Sexual Abuse, Physical Abuse & Neglect in Maternally Neglected Children', in *Canadian Journal of Public Health*, no. 3, pp 15–26.

Barnardo's (1995) *Streets & Lanes (SALs), Annual Report.* London: Barnardo's.

Barrett, D. (1994) 'Social Work on the Street: Responding to Juvenile Prostitution in Amsterdam, London & Paris', in *Social Work in Europe*, vol. 1, no. 1, pp 29–32.

Barrett, D. (1995) 'Child Prostitution', in *Highlight*, no. 135. London: National Children's Bureau.

Barrett, D. & Beckett, W. (1996) 'Health Promoting Itself: Reaching Out to Children Who Sell Sex to Survive', in the *British Journal of Nursing*, vol. 5, no. 18, pp 1128–1129.

Barry, K. (1995) 'The Prostitution of Sexuality', in *Journal of Sex Research*, vol. 32, issue 2, pp 172–174.

Benjamin, H. (1964) *Prostitution and Morality.* Julian Press.

Bloor, M., McKeganey, N. & Barnard, M. (1990) 'An Ethnographic Study of HIV-related Risk Practices Among Glasgow Rent Boys and Their Clients: Report of a Pilot Study', in *AIDS Care*, vol. 2, no. 1, pp17–24.

Boswell, J. (1980) *Christianity, Social Tolerance & Homosexuality*. Chicago UCP.

Boyer, Debra (1989) 'Male Prostitution & Homosexual Identity', in *Journal of Homosexuality*, vol. 17, pp 151–184.

Butts, William (1947) 'Boy Prostitutes of the Metropolis', in *Journal of Clinical Psychopathology*, vol. 8, pp 674–681.

Byrne, Suzy & Larkin, Junior (1994) *Coming Out*. Martello Books.

Calhoun, Thomas & Pickernill, Brian (1988) 'Young Male Prostitutes: Their Knowledge of Selected Sexually Transmitted Diseases', in *Psychology*, vol. 25, pp 1–8.

Cates, A. Jim (1989) 'Adolescent Male Prostitution by Choice', in *Child and Adolescent Social Work*, vol. 6, no. 2, pp 151–156.

Cockrell, J. & Hoffman, D. (1989) 'Identifying the Needs of Boys at Risk in Prostitution', in *Social Work Today*, vol. 20, no. 36, pp 20–21.

Coleman, Eli (1989) 'The Development of Male Prostitution Activity among Gay and Bisexual Adolescents', in *Journal of Homosexuality*, vol.17, pp 131–149.

Cory, D.W. & Leroy, J. P. (1963) *The Homosexual & His Society: A view from within New York*. Citadel.

Coutinho, A., Roel (1988) 'Role of Male Prostitutes in Spread of Sexually Transmitted Disease and Human Immuno-Deficiency Virus', in *Genitourinary Medicine*, vol. 64, pp 207–208.

Craft, M. (1966) 'Boy Prostitutes & Their Fate', in *British Journal of Psychiatry*, vol. 112, pp 1111–1114.

Criminal Law (Sexual Offences) Act, 1993

Cunningham, Su (1980) 'Some Aspects of Prostitution in the West End of London in 1979', in *Sex Offenders in the Criminal Justice System*, pp 121–131.

Davidson, Michael (1968) *Some Boys: A Homosexual Odyssey*. The Garden City Press Ltd.

Davies, P. M. & Simpson, P. J. (1987) *On Contemporary forms of Male Homosexual Prostitution in London.* Social Research Unit, University College Cardiff.

Dietz, Elliott, Park (1978) 'Male Homosexual Prostitution', in *Bulletin of the American Academy of Psychology*, vol. 6, pp 468–471.

Dublin Lesbian & Gay Men's Collectives (1986) *Out For Ourselves – The Lives of Irish Lesbian & Gay Men.* Dublin Lesbian & Gay Men's Collectives.

Ennew, J. (1986) *The Sexual Exploitation of Children.* Cambridge: Polity Press.

Fisher, B., Weisbert, H. & Marotta, T. (1982) *Report on Adolescent Male Prostitution.* San Francisco, California: Urban & Rural Systems Associates.

Foster, Claire (1991) 'Male Youth Prostitution: Perspectives, Policy & Practice', in *Social Work Monographs.* Norwich.

Friedman, R. et al. (1998) 'Drug Scene Roles & HIV Risk', in *Addiction*, vol. 93, no.9, pp 1403–1416.

Gangoli, Geetanjali (1998) 'Prostitution, Legalisation and Decriminalisation' in *Economic & Political Weekly*, March 7, pp 504–505.

Gay Men's Health Project (1997) *Men in Prostitution,* compiled by AnnMarie O'Connor, Women's Education Research & Resource Centre UCD, Dublin.

Gibson, B. (1995) *Male Order*, London: Cassell plc.

Goldstein, P. J. (1979) *Prostitution & Drugs*, Lexington Books.

Green, J. (1992) *It's no Game*, Leicester National Youth Agency.

Hanslope, J. & Waite, M. (1994) 'Safer on the Streets', in *Health Lines*, vol. 10, pp 20–1.

Harris, M. (1973) *The Dilly Boys: Male Prostitution in Piccadilly*, London, Croom Helm.

Heinz, K. (1992) 'Adolescents at Risk from HIV Infection', in R. J. DiClemente (ed.) *Adolescents and AIDS*. Newbury Park, California: Sage Publications.

Jaget, C. (ed.) (1980) *Prostitutes: Our Life*. London: Falling Wall Press.

Jay, K. & Young, A. (1979) *The Gay Report*. New York: Summit Books.

Joseph, C. (1995) 'Scarlet Wounding: Issues of Child Prostitution', in *Journal of Psychohistory*, vol. 23, no.1, pp 2–17.

Kenny, Fr Kevin (1988) *It Only Hurts When I Grow – Stories from Covenant House for Hurting Kids*. Paulist Press.

Kjeldsen, Mark (1988, 1989) *Streetwise Youth: Outreach Work with Young Men Involved in the 'Rent Scene' of Central London* London: Barnado's, .

Kufeldt, K. (1991) 'Social Policy & Runaways', in *Journal of Health & Social Policy*, vol. 2, no. 4, pp 37–49.

Lee, M. & O'Brien, R. (1995) *The Game's Up: Redefining Child Prostitution*. London: The Children's Society.

Lloyd, Robin (1979) *Playland – A Study of Human Exploitation*. Quartet Books Ltd.

McCarthy, B. & Hagan, J. (1992) 'Surviving on the Street: The Experience of Homeless Youth', in *Journal of*

Adolescent Research, vol. 7, no. 4, pp 412–430.

McCormack, M. et al. (1986) 'Runaway Youths and Sexual Victimisation: Gender Differences in an Adolescent Runaway Population', in *Child Abuse and Neglect*, vol.10, no. 3, pp 387–395.

McDonnell, R. J. et al. (1988)– 'Health Risk Profile of Prostitutes in Dublin', in *International Journal of STD & AIDS*, vol. 9, pp 485–488.

McGeady, Mary Rose Sr. (1993) *'God Isn't Done with Me Yet': The Unforgettable Story of America's Homeless Kids.* Covenant House.

McMullen, Richie J. (1987) 'Youth Prostitution: A Balance of Power', in *Journal of Adolescence*, vol. 10, pp 35–43.

McMullen, Richie J. (1990) *Enchanted Youth.* GMP Publisher Ltd.

McNamara, R. P. (1996) 'The Times Square Hustler: Male Prostitution in New York City', in *Social Forces*, vol. 75, Issue 1, pp 395–396.

Matthews, F. (1987) *Familiar Strangers: A Study of Adolescent Prostitution.* Toronto: Central Toronto Youth Services.

Mendel Parynik, Matthew (1995) *The Male Survivor: The Impact of Sexual Abuse.* Sage Publications Inc.

Naden, M. Susan et al. (1998) 'Antecedents to Prostitution', in *Journal of Interpersonal Violence,* vol. 13, no. 2, pp 206–221.

O'Connor, AnnMarie (1996) *Women Working in Prostitution: Towards a Healthier Future,* prepared for EURO-PAP & the Eastern Health Board (Women's Health Project).

O'Connor, Art (1996) *Criminals: Inside the Minds of Criminals & Victims.* Dublin: Marino Books.

Plummer, Kenneth (1981) *The Making of the Modern Homosexual.* Hutchinson & Co. Ltd.

Robinson, T. (1989) 'London's Homosexual Male Prostitutes: Power, Peer Groups & HIV' in *Sigma Working Papers*, no. 12. London: South Bank Polytechnic.

Sanderson, Terry (1996) *A Stranger in the Family: How to Cope if Your Child Is Gay.* The Other Way Press.

Scambler, G. (1998) 'Rethinking Prostitution: Purchasing Sex in the 1990s', in *British Journal of Criminology*, vol. 38, issue 2, pp 335–336.

Segal, L. (1990) *Slow Motion: Changing Masculinities, Changing Men.* London: Virago Press.

Seng, M. (1989) 'Child Sexual Abuse and Adolescent Prostitution: A comparative Study', in *Adolescence*, vol. 24, no. 95, pp 665–675.

Sereny, G. (1984) *The Invisible Children: Child Prostitution in America, Germany and Britain.* London: André Deutsch.

Shaw, Ian & Butler, Ian (1988) 'Understanding Young People and Prostitution: A Foundation for Practice?' in *British Journal of Social Work*, pp 177–196.

Silbert, M. & Pines, A. (1981) 'Sexual Child Abuse as an Antecedent to Prostitution', in *Child Abuse & Neglect*, vol. 5, pp 407–411.

Sweetman, Rosita (1979) *On Our Backs: Sexual Attitudes in a Changing Ireland.* London: Pan Books Ltd.

Tamsin, Wilton (1997) *En-Gendering AIDS: Deconstructing Sex, Text & Epidemic.* Sage Publications Ltd.

Unger, B., Jennifer et al.(1988)'Early Adolescent Street Youth: An Overlooked Population with Unique Problems and Service Needs', in *Journal of Early Adolescence*, vol. 18, no. 4, pp 325–348.

Walkowitz, R. Judith (1980) *Prostitution & Victorian Society: Women, Class & State*. Cambridge University Press.

Weisberg, D. K. (1985) *Children of the Night: A Study of Adolescent Prostitution*. Massachusetts: Lexington Books.

Weldorf D. & Murphy, S.(1990) 'Intravenous Drug Use & Syringe-sharing Practices of Call Men & Hustlers', in M. Plant (ed.) *AIDS, Drugs & Prostitution*. London: Travistock/Routledge.

West, D. & DeVillers, B. (1992) *Male Prostitution: Gay Sex Services in London*. London: Duckworth.

West, D. J. (1994) *'Male Prostitution'* in *Contemporary Sociology – A Journal of Reviews*, vol. 23, issue 6, pp 856–859.

West, D. J. (1968) *Homosexuality*, London, Duckworth.

White, D. et al. (1993) 'Sexual Issues & Condom Use Among Injecting Drug Users', in *AIDS Care*, vol. 5, no. 4, pp 427–433.

Yates, G., MacKenzie, R., Pennbridge, J. & Swofford, A. (1991) 'A Risk Profile Comparison of Homeless Youth Involved in Prostitution and Homeless Youth not Involved', in *Journal of Adolescent Health*, vol. 12, no. 7, pp 545–548.

Zgourides, Georges (1996) *Human Sexuality: Contemporary Perspectives*. University of Portland: Harper Collins College Publishers.

Corcoran, Jason 'Illicit Sex in the Ilac', the *Evening Herald*, 19 April 1999.

Davies, N. 'Children of the Night', the *Guardian*, 29 August 1994.

Lambert, Bruce 'AIDS Among Prostitutes Not as Prevalent as Believed, Studies Show', the *New York Times*, 20 September 1988.

Londodale, S. 'Unfair Play on the Game' in the *Independent*, 31 July 1994.

Gay Times, October 1998, January–June 1999

Hot Press, January–June 1999

H&E (naturist magazine), May 1998, December 1998, Summer Quarterly 1999

In Dublin, January–June 1999

INTERNET WEBSITES

http://www.amoc.demon.nl/enmp/description.htm
http://www.walnet.org/osis/groups/swav/swav.html
http://www.bayswan.org/male.html
http://www.bayswan.org/diverse.html
http://www.bayswan.org
http://www.virtualcity.com
http://www.bayswan.org/Trans.html
http://www.wam.umd.edu/~mariecug.ac/html
http://www.walnet.org/osis/groups/swav/swav.html
http://www.walnet.org/osis/news
http://www.walnet.org/osis/usa-82/numbers-8211.html
http://www.dtl.org/article/homosexuals.htm

http://www.bayswan.org/COSW.html
http://www.irish-times.com